LEARN TO

Knit for Baby

Spun Sugar Baby Set, page 83

www.companyscoming.com
visit our website

TABLE OF CONTENTS

Feeling Crafty? Get Creative! 6 • Foreword 7 • Knitting Basics 8

Cuddly Baby Blankets & More

Knit a soft blanket for a special baby and add a wash cloth, block or cap to match.

Just Ducky Blankie, page 36

Rainbow Blanket, page 30

Garter Stripes Ensemble, page 72

Little Buttercup Baby Cap, page 98

TABLE OF CONTENTS

Layettes for Baby

Give a unique gift of a matching baby set which includes a sweet sweater, hat and booties.

The Best-Dressed Baby

Try your hand at knitting rompers, jackets, caps and socks to make your baby the best-dressed.

Bundles of Joy, page 39

On-the-Go Baby Set, page 78

Striped Henley Romper Set, page 93

Precious Baby Jacket & Cube, page 88

Feeling Crafty? Get Creative!

Each 160-page book features easy-to-follow, step-by-step instructions and full-page colour photographs of every project. Whatever your crafting fancy, there's a Company's Coming Creative Series craft book to match!

Beading: Beautiful Accessories in Under an Hour

Complement your wardrobe, give your home extra flair or add an extra-special personal touch to gifts with these quick and easy beading projects. Create any one of these special crafts in an hour or less.

Knitting: Easy Fun for Everyone

Take a couple of needles and some yarn and see what beautiful things you can make! Learn how to make fashionable sweaters, comfy knitted blankets, scarves, bags and other knitted crafts with these easy to intermediate knitting patterns.

Card Making: Handmade Greetings for All Occasions

Making your own cards is a fun, creative and inexpensive way of letting someone know you care. Stamp, emboss, quill or layer designs in a creative and unique card with your own personal message for friends or family.

Patchwork Quilting

In this book full of throws, baby quilts, table toppers, wall hangings—and more—you'll find plenty of beautiful projects to try. With the modern fabrics available, and the many practical and decorative applications, patchwork quilting is not just for Grandma!

Crocheting: Easy Blankets, Throws & Wraps

Find projects perfect for decorating your home, for looking great while staying warm or for giving that one-of-a-kind gift. A range of simple but stunning designs make crocheting quick, easy and entertaining.

Sewing: Fun Weekend Projects

Find a wide assortment of easy and attractive projects to help you create practical storage solutions, decorations for any room or just the right gift for that someone special. Create table runners, placemats, baby quilts, pillows and more!

For more information about Company's Coming craft books, visit our website, www.companyscoming.com

FOREWORD

If you have seen knitters busily creating lovely items for the babies and toddlers of family and friends and wanted to join in, then wait no longer. Now is the time to join in the fun and discover how rewarding it can be to knit for baby. To make picking up this popular needlecraft easy, we've included a 17-page how-to section with over 60 illustrations and colour photos along with step-by-step instructions. Included are all the basic stitches as well as many additional stitches, techniques and tips you will need to develop your knitting skills. If you haven't held a knitting needle recently, these instructions will provide a refresher course that will soon have you joyfully knitting again.

A good way to start is by knitting a baby blanket—because there is no shaping, they are easy to knit and they are much smaller than a regular afghan so they take much less time. Along with cuddly baby blankets, this section of the book has a variety of gift ideas. Choose from blankets with matching hats and booties, washcloths, a bottle cozy, a pacifier holder and baby blocks. All these projects would be well-received gifts by mother and baby alike.

For those knitters who have a little more time, we introduce baby layettes. Each set has three or four coordinated projects. Many of the sets have a blanket, sweater, hat or cap and booties, all to match. Baby will look sweet as can be in his or her matching set. Once you learn the stitch pattern when knitting the baby afghan, you can quickly stitch the sweater or cap to match. With each piece you knit, the pattern becomes easier.

To make the special baby in your life the best-dressed, you'll want to try your hand at knitting rompers, dresses, jackets, cardigans, pullovers, socks and hoodies. Each stitch you knit will be filled with love for the precious babies and toddlers who will be receiving these pieces. Many knitters start out by knitting for babies, and it is a skill you can use all your life—whether you are knitting for your child, grandchild or the grandchild of your neighbour.

Once you knit the first piece, you will discover how relaxing, fun and easy it is to knit lovely baby items.

All the projects in this book are knit-friendly, with many beginner and easy projects, as well as a few for intermediate knitters. Enjoy each stitch as you knit for baby!

Patchwork Checks, page 32

KNITTING BASICS

Getting Started

Supplies Needed for Practice Lessons:

One 3½ oz skein of knitting worsted weight yarn in a
    light colour
Size 8 (5mm) 10-inch long straight knitting needles
Size H/8/5mm crochet hook (for repairs)
Scissors
Tape measure
Size 16 tapestry needle or plastic yarn needle

To knit, you need only a pair of knitting needles, some
yarn, a pair of scissors, a tape measure, a crochet hook and
a tapestry or yarn needle. Later on, for some of the projects
in this book, you can add all kinds of accessories such as
markers, stitch holders and needle point protectors. But for
now, you only need the items listed above.

Yarn

Yarn comes in a wonderful selection of fibres, ranging
from wool to metallic; textures from lumpy to smooth;
colours from the palest pastels to vibrant neon shades;
and weights from gossamer fine to chunky.

The most commonly used yarn, and the one you'll need
for the lessons in this book, is worsted weight (sometimes
called 4-ply). It is readily available in a wide variety of
beautiful colours. Choose a light colour for practice—it
will be much easier to see the individual stitches.

Always read yarn labels carefully for information including
the following: how much yarn is in the skein, hank or ball,
in ounces or grams and in yards or meters; the type of
yarn; how to care for it; and sometimes how to pull the
yarn from the skein (and yes, there is a trick to this!). The
label usually bears a dye lot number, which assures you
that the colour of each skein with this same number is
identical. The same colour may vary from dye lot to dye
lot, creating unsightly variations in colour when a project
is finished—so when purchasing yarn for a project, be sure
to match the dye lot number on the skeins and purchase
enough to complete the project.

You'll need a blunt-pointed sewing needle, with an eye big
enough to carry the yarn, for weaving in ends and joining
pieces. You can use a size 16 steel tapestry needle, or
purchase a large plastic sewing needle called a yarn needle.

Crochet Hooks

Even though you're knitting, not crocheting, you'll need to
have a crochet hook handy for correcting mistakes, retrieving
dropped stitches and for some finishing techniques. (You
don't need to know how to crochet, though!)

The hook size you need depends on the thickness of the
yarn you are using for your project, and on the size of the
knitting needles.

Here's a handy chart to show you what size hook to use:

Knitting Needle Size	Crochet Hook Size
5, 6	F
7, 8, 9	G
10 and 10½	H
11 and 13	I
15 and 17	J

Knitting Needles

Knitting needles come in pairs of straight needles, each having a shaped point at one end and a knob at the other end so that the stitches won't slide off. Needles also come in sets of four double-pointed needles used for making small seamless projects, and in circular form with a point at each end.

You will most often use straight needles, which are readily available in many materials including aluminum, bamboo and plastic. The straight needles come in a variety of lengths, the most common being 10 inches and 14 inches. For our lessons, we will use the 10-inch length.

The needles also come in a variety of sizes, which refer to the diameter and thus the size of the stitch you can make with them. These are numbered from 0 (the smallest usually available) to 17 (the largest usually available). There are larger needles, but they are not used as often. For our lessons, we use a size 8 needle, an average size for use with worsted weight yarn.

Let's look at a knitting needle:

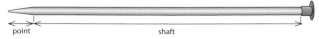

point   shaft

Now, with your yarn and needles ready, let's get started.

Lesson 1

Casting On

Knitting always starts with a row of foundation stitches worked onto one needle. Making a foundation row is called casting on. Although there are several ways of casting on, the following way is the easiest for beginners:

1. Make a slip knot on one needle as follows: Make a yarn loop, leaving about 4-inch length of yarn at free end.

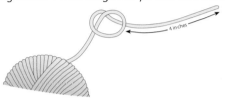

Insert knitting needle into loop and draw up yarn from free end to make a loop on needle.

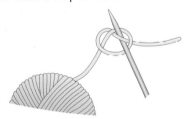

Pull yarn firmly, but not tightly, to form a slip knot on the shaft, not the point, of the needle. Pull yarn end to tighten the loop. This slip knot counts as your first stitch.

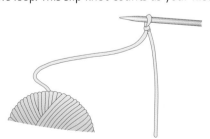

2. Place the needle with the knot in your left hand, placing the thumb and index finger close to the point of the needle, which helps you control it.

3. Hold the other needle with your right hand, again with your fingers close to the point. Grasp the needle firmly, but not tightly.

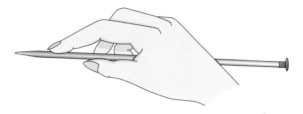

4. Your right hand controls the yarn coming from the ball. To help keep your tension even, hold the yarn loosely against the palm of your hand with three fingers, then up and over your index finger. These diagrams show how this looks from above the hand and beneath the hand.

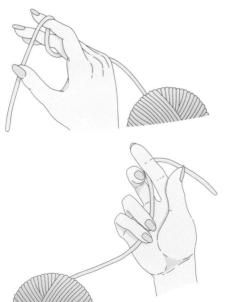

5. Insert the point of the right needle—from front to back—into the slip knot and under the left needle.

6. Continuing to hold left needle in your left hand, move left fingers over to brace right needle.

With right index finger, pick up the yarn from the ball,

and releasing right hand's grip on the right needle, bring yarn under and over the point of right needle.

7. Returning right fingers to right needle, draw yarn through stitch with right needle.

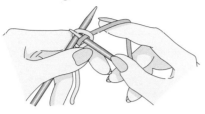

8. Slide left needle point into new stitch, then remove right needle.

9. Pull ball of yarn gently, but not tightly, to make stitch snug on needle; you should be able to slip the stitch back and forth on the shaft of the needle easily.

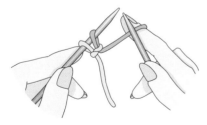

You have now made one stitch, and there are two stitches on left needle (remember the slip knot counts as a stitch).

10. Insert point of right needle—from front to back—into stitch you've just made and under left needle.

Repeat Steps 6 through 10 for next stitch.

Continue repeating Steps 6 through 10 until you have 24 stitches on the left needle. Be sure to pull each stitch up, off the point and onto the shaft of the left needle.

Lesson 2

The Knit Stitch

All knitting is made up of only two basic stitches, the knit stitch and the purl stitch. These are combined in many ways to create different effects and textures. That means you're halfway to being a knitter, since you already learned the knit stitch as you practiced casting on! The first three steps of the knit stitch are exactly like casting on.

1. Hold the needle with the 24 cast-on stitches from Lesson 1 in your left hand. Insert the point of the right needle in the first stitch, from front to back, just as in casting on.

2. With right index finger, bring yarn from the skein under and over the point of the right needle.

3. Draw yarn through the stitch with the right needle point.

4. The next step now differs from casting on. Slip the loop on the left needle off, so the new stitch is entirely on the right needle.

Now you've completed your first knit stitch! Repeat these four steps in each stitch remaining on the left needle. When all stitches are on the right needle and the left needle is free, another row has been completed. Turn the right needle and place it in your left hand. Hold the free needle in your right hand. Work another row of stitches in same manner as last row, taking care not to work too tightly. Work 10 more rows of knit stitches.

The pattern formed by knitting every row is called garter stitch and looks the same on both sides. When counting rows in garter stitch, each raised ridge indicates you have knitted two rows.

Hint: When working on a garter stitch project it is helpful to place a small safety pin on the right side of the piece, as after a few rows both sides look the same.

Lesson 3

The Purl Stitch

The reverse of the knit stitch is called the purl stitch. Instead of inserting the right needle point from front to back under the left needle (as you did for the knit stitch), you will now insert it from back to front, in front of the left needle. Work as follows on the 24 stitches already on your needle.

1. Insert the right needle, from right to left, into the first stitch and in front of the left needle.

2. Holding the yarn in front of the work (side toward you), bring it around the right needle counterclockwise.

3. With the right needle, pull the yarn back through the stitch.

4. Slide the stitch off the left needle, leaving the new stitch on the right needle.

Your first purl stitch is now completed. Continue to repeat these three steps in every stitch across the row. The row you have just purled will be considered the wrong side of your work for the moment.

Now transfer the needle with the stitches from your right to left hand; the side of the work now facing you is called the right side of your work. Knit every stitch in the row; at end of row, transfer the needle with the stitches to your left hand, then purl every stitch in the row. Knit across another row, purl across another row.

Now stop and look at your work; by alternating knit and purl rows, you are creating one of the most frequently used stitch patterns in knitting, *stockinette stitch*.

Turn the work over to the right side; it should look like stitches in Photo A. The wrong side of the work should look like stitches in Photo B.

Photo A

Photo B

Continue with your practice piece, alternately knitting and purling rows, until you feel comfortable with the needles and yarn. As you work you'll see that your piece will begin to look more even.

Hint: Hold your work and hands in a comfortable relaxed position. The more comfortable and relaxed you are, the more even your work will be.

Lesson 4

Correcting Mistakes
Dropped Stitches
Each time you knit or purl a stitch, take care to pull the stitch off the left needle after completing the new stitch. Otherwise, you will be adding stitches when you don't want to. If you let a stitch slip off the needle before you've knitted or purled it, it's called a dropped stitch. Even expert knitters drop a stitch now and then, but a dropped stitch must be picked up and put back on the needle. If not, the stitch will "run" down the length of the piece, just like a run in a stocking!

If you notice the dropped stitch right away, and it has not run down more than one row, you can usually place it back on the needle easily.

But, if it has dropped several rows, you'll find it easier to use a crochet hook to work the stitch back up to the needle.

On the knit side (right side of work) of the stockinette stitch, insert the crochet hook into the dropped stitch from front to back, under the horizontal strand in the row above.

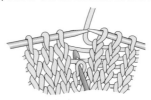

Hook the horizontal strand above and pull through the loop on the crochet hook. Continue in this manner until you reach the last row worked, then transfer the loop from the crochet hook to the left needle, being careful not to twist it.

Unravelling Stitches

Sometimes it is necessary to unravel a large number of stitches, even down several rows, to correct a mistake. Whenever possible, carefully unravel the stitches one by one by putting the needle into the row below and undoing the stitch above, until the mistake is reached.

If several rows need to be unravelled, carefully slide all stitches off the needle and unravel each row down to the row in which the error occurred. Then unravel this row, stitch by stitch, placing each stitch, without twisting it, back on the needle in the correct position.

Lesson 5

Binding Off

Now you've learned how to cast on, knit and purl the stitches; next, you need to know how to take the stitches off the needle once you've finished a piece.

The process used to secure the stitches is called binding off. Let's bind off your practice piece; be careful to work loosely for this procedure, and begin with the right side (the knit side) of your work facing you.

Knit Bind-Off

1. Knit the first two stitches. Now insert the left needle into the first of the two stitches, the one you knitted first,

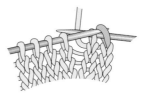

and pull it over the second stitch and completely off the needle. You have now bound off one stitch.

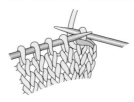

2. Knit one more stitch; insert the left needle into the first stitch on the right needle and pull the first stitch over the new stitch and completely off the needle. Another stitch is now bound off.

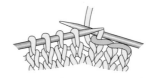

Repeat Step 2 four times more; now knit each of the remaining stitches on the left needle. You should have 18 stitches on the right needle, and you have bound off six stitches on the knit side of your work. *Note: The first of the 18 stitches was worked while binding off the last stitch at the beginning of the row.*

To bind off on the purl side, turn your practice piece so the wrong side of your work is facing you.

Purl Bind–Off

1. Purl the first two stitches. Now insert the left needle into the first stitch on the right needle,

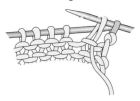

and pull it over the 2nd stitch and completely off the needle. You have now bound off one stitch.

2. Purl one more stitch; insert the left needle into the first stitch on the right needle and pull the first stitch over the new stitch and completely off the needle. Another stitch is bound off.

Repeat Step 2 four times more; now purl each of the 11 stitches remaining on the left needle for a total of 12 stitches on the right needle.

Turn your work so that the right side is facing you; bind off six stitches in the same manner that you bound off the first six stitches on this side, then knit remaining stitches.

Turn your work and bind off the remaining stitches on the wrong side; there will be one stitch left on the needle and you are ready to "finish off" or "end off" the yarn. To do this,

cut the yarn leaving about a 6-inch end. With the needle, draw this end up through the final stitch to secure it.

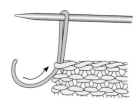

You have just learned to bind off knit stitches on the right side of your work and purl stitches on the wrong side of your work. When you wish to bind off in a pattern stitch, where some stitches in a row have been knitted and others purled, knit the knit stitches and purl the purl stitches as you work across the row.

Always bind off loosely to maintain the same amount of stretch or "give" at the edge as in the rest of your work. If the bind off is too tight at the neckband ribbing of a pullover sweater, for example, the sweater will not fit over your head!

Hint: You can ensure the binding off being loose enough if you replace the needle in your right hand with a needle one size larger.

Lesson 6

Increasing

To shape knitted pieces, you will make them wider or narrower by increasing or decreasing a certain number of stitches from time to time.

Begin a new practice piece by casting on 12 stitches. Work four rows of garter stitch (remember this means you will knit every row); then on the next row, purl across (this purl side now becomes the wrong side of the work, since you will now begin working in stockinette stitch). Knit one more row, then purl one more row. You are now ready to practice increasing.

Although there are many ways to increase, this method is used most often.

Knit (or Purl) Two Stitches in One

1. On your practice piece (with the right side facing you), work as follows in the first stitch:

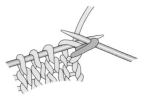

2. Insert the tip of the right needle from front to back into the stitch, and knit it in the usual manner but don't remove the stitch from the left needle.

Insert the needle (from front to back) into the back loop of the same stitch, and knit it again, this time slipping the stitch off the left needle. You have now increased one stitch.

Knit across the row until one stitch remains, then increase again by repeating Steps 1 and 2. You should now have 14 stitches.

Purl one row then knit one row, without increasing.

On your next row, the purl side, again increase in the first stitch. To increase on the purl side, insert the needle (from back to front) into the stitch; purl the stitch in the usual manner but don't remove it from the left needle. Then insert the needle (from back to front) into the back loop of the same stitch;

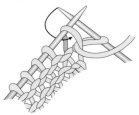

purl it again, this time slipping the stitch off. Then purl across to the last stitch; increase again. You should now have 16 stitches.

Now knit one row and purl one row without increasing.

Lesson 7

Decreasing
Method 1: Right Slanting Decrease
Knit (or Purl) Two Stitches Together
In this method, you simply knit two stitches as one. Knit the first stitch on your practice piece, then decrease as follows:

1. Insert the needle in usual manner but through the fronts of the next two stitches on the left needle.

2. Bring yarn under and over the point of the needle,

draw the yarn through both stitches,

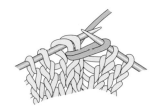

slip the stitches off the left needle and one new stitch will be on the right needle.

You have decreased one stitch. Knit across to the last three stitches; repeat Steps 1 and 2 again to decrease another stitch, then knit the last stitch. You should now have 14 stitches.

This decrease can also be worked on the purl side. On the next row of your practice piece, purl one stitch, then insert the needle in the fronts of next two stitches and purl them as if they were one stitch. Purl to the last three stitches, decrease again; purl remaining stitch.

Method 2: Left Slanting Decrease
Pass Slipped Stitch Over

This method is often used in the shaping of raglans or other pieces where a definite decrease line is desired. In the following samples the decrease is worked one stitch in from the edge. By working in one stitch from the edge, the decrease does not become a part of the seam.

To use this method you must first know how to "slip" a stitch. When instructions say to slip a stitch, this means you will slip it from the left needle to the right, without working it. To do this, insert right needle into the stitch as if you were going to purl it (even if it's a knit stitch); but instead of purling, slip the stitch from the left needle to the right needle.

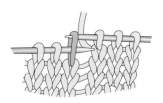

Note: Always insert the needle as to purl when slipping a stitch, unless instructions specify "slip as to knit"; in that case, insert the needle in the position for knitting, and slip the stitch in the same manner.

Now that you know how to slip a stitch, you can practice the second method of decreasing. On your practice piece, knit the first stitch. Instructions to decrease may read: "Slip 1, knit 1, pass slipped stitch over." To do this, work as follows:

1. Slip the next stitch, as to purl.

2. Knit the next stitch.

3. Pass the slipped stitch over the knitted stitch by using point of the left needle to lift the slipped stitch over the next stitch and completely off the needle.

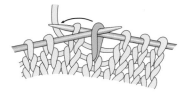

Knit to the last three stitches. Repeat Steps 1, 2 and 3. Then knit the last stitch.

This decrease can also be worked on the purl side. To do so, purl the first stitch. Slip next stitch, purl the next stitch, pass slipped stitch over purled stitch. Purl to the last three stitches, then repeat the purl decrease and purl the last stitch.

Hint: When slipping stitches the yarn is not moved unless specified in the instructions.

Decreasing, Alternate Method 2: Left Slanting Decrease
Slip, Slip, Knit
This decrease is similar in appearance to the previous method but has a smoother look as the stitch is not lifted or pulled up causing a slightly larger loop.

When this decrease is used the stitches are slipped as if to **knit** (see Note on page 17).

1. To practice this method, knit the first stitch, slip the next two stitches one at a time from the left to the right needle as if to knit.

2. Insert the left needle into the front of both stitches, bring the yarn around the needle as if knitting and lift the two stitches over and off the needle at the same time.

Knit to the last three stitches, repeat the slip, slip, knit the two slipped stitches together, then knit the last stitch. Purl one row.

Notice the two methods of decreasing. Method 1 causes the decreased stitch to slant from left to right, while in Method 2 the stitch slants from right to left. For a sweater, both methods are often used in the same row for a mirrored effect.

To practice this mirrored look, knit one stitch, decrease using either of the Method 2 decreases, knit to the last three stitches, knit two stitches together using Method 1 and knit the last stitch. Notice that both decreases slant towards the centre of your sample.

Lesson 8

Ribbing
Sometimes you want a piece of knitting to fit more closely—such as at the neck, wrists or bottom of a sweater. To do this, a combination of knit and purl stitches alternating in the same row, called ribbing, creates an elastic effect. To practice ribbing, start a new piece by casting on 24 stitches loosely. Always cast on loosely for ribbing, to provide enough stretch in the first row.

Knit Two, Purl Two Ribbing
Pattern Row: Knit two stitches, then bring yarn under the needle to the front of the work and purl two stitches; take the yarn under the needle to the back of the work and knit two stitches; yarn to front again, purl two stitches.

Note: You may tend to add stitches accidentally by forgetting to move the yarn to the front before purling, or to the back before knitting.

Remembering to move the yarn, repeat this knit two, purl two alternating pattern across the row.

Work this same Pattern Row 11 more times or until you feel comfortable with it. Your work should look like this:

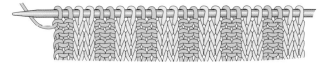

Hint: If you have trouble distinguishing a knit stitch or a purl stitch, remember that the smooth "v-shaped" stitches are knit stitches and the bumpy ones are purl stitches.

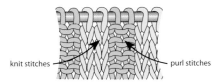

knit stitches   purl stitches

Bind off loosely, remembering to knit the knit stitches and purl the purl stitches. Look at the work and see how the ribbing draws it in.

Knit One, Purl One Ribbing

This rib stitch pattern produces a finer ribbing, and is often used on baby clothes or on garments knitted with light weight yarns. Again cast on 24 stitches.

Pattern Row: Knit the first stitch, yarn under needle to front, purl the next stitch; yarn under needle to back, knit next stitch; yarn to front, purl next stitch. Continue across row, alternating one knit stitch with one purl stitch.

Work this same Pattern Row 11 more times or until you feel comfortable with this rib pattern. Your work should look like this:

Practice this ribbing for several more rows, then bind off in ribbing, knitting the knit (smooth) stitches and purling the purl (bumpy) stitches.

Lesson 9

Changing Yarn
Joining Yarn

New yarn should be added only at the beginning of a row, never in the middle of a row, unless this is required for a colour pattern change. To add yarn, tie the new strand around the old strand, making a knot at the edge of work, leaving at least a 4-inch end on both old and new strands. Then proceed to knit with the new yarn. The ends will be hidden later.

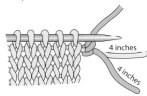

4 inches

4 inches

Carrying Yarn

When a yarn is repeated every several rows, it can be carried along the edge when not in use. At the beginning of the row, bring the carried colour under and over the colour just used and begin knitting (or purling).

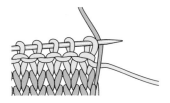

Lesson 10

Gauge and Measuring

This is the most important lesson of all, for if you don't work to gauge, your knitted garments will not fit as designed.

Gauge simply means the number of stitches per inch and the number of rows per inch, that result from a specified yarn worked with needles in a specified size. This was the information used by the designer when creating the project.

But, since everyone knits differently—some loosely, some tightly, some in between—the measurements of individual work will vary greatly, even when the knitters use exactly the same pattern and exactly the same size yarn and needles.

That's why you need to knit a gauge swatch before you actually start working on a project.

Needle sizes given in instructions are merely guides and should never be used without making a 4-inch square sample swatch to check your gauge. *It is your responsibility to make sure you achieve the gauge specified in the pattern.* To achieve this gauge, you may need to use a different needle size—either larger or smaller—than that specified in the pattern. Always change to larger or smaller needles if necessary to achieve gauge.

Here's how to check your gauge. At the beginning of every knit pattern you'll find a gauge given, like this (note the use of abbreviations):

Gauge

16 sts and 24 rows = 4 inches/10cm in stockinette st, with size 8 needles

This means that you will work your gauge swatch in stockinette stitch, and will try to achieve a gauge of 16 stitches and 24 rows to 4 inches. You must make a gauge swatch at least 4 inches square to adequately test your work.

Starting with the recommended size 8 needle, cast on 16 stitches. Work in stockinette stitch for 24 rows. Loosely bind off all stitches.

Place the swatch on a flat surface and pin it out, being careful not to stretch it. Measure the outside edges; the swatch should be 4 inches square.

Now measure the centre 2 inches from side to side, and count the actual stitches. There should be eight stitches in the 2 inches.

8 stitches = 2 inches

Then measure the centre 2 inches from top to bottom and count the rows per inch. There should be 12 rows in the 2 inches.

12 rows = 2 inches

If you have more stitches or rows per inch than specified, make another swatch with a size larger needles.

If you have fewer stitches or rows per inch than specified, make another swatch with a size smaller needles.

Making gauge swatches before beginning a garment takes time and is a bother. But if you don't make the effort to do this important step, you'll never be able to create attractive, well-fitting garments.

Once you've begun a garment, it's a good idea to keep checking your gauge every few inches; if you become relaxed, you may find yourself knitting more loosely; if you tense up, your knitting may become tighter. To keep your gauge, it may be necessary to change needle sizes in the middle of a garment.

For a swatch in garter stitch, every two rows form a ridge which needs to be taken into consideration when counting rows.

2 rows

Hint: Sometimes you'll find that you have the correct stitch gauge, but can't get the row gauge even with a change in needle size. If so, the stitch gauge is more important than the row gauge, with one exception: raglan sweaters. In knitting raglans, the armhole depth is based on row gauge, so you must achieve both stitch and row gauge.

Lesson 11

Reading Patterns
Knitting patterns are written in a special language, full of abbreviations, asterisks, parentheses, and other symbols and terms. These short forms are used so instructions will not take up too much space. They may seem confusing at first, but once understood, they are easy to follow.

Symbols
[ ] work instructions within brackets as many times as directed such as [k2, p2] twice.

* repeat instructions following the * as directed; thus, "rep from * twice" means after working the instructions once, repeat the instructions following the asterisk twice more (three times in all).

( ) parentheses are used to list the garment sizes and to provide additional information to clarify instructions.

Work in pattern as established is usually used when referring to a pattern stitch. The term means to continue following the pattern stitch as it is set up (established) on the needle. Work any subsequent increases or decreases in such a way that the established pattern remains the same (usually, working added stitches at the beginning or end of a row), outside the established pattern area.

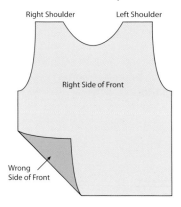

Right Shoulder   Left Shoulder

Right Side of Front

Wrong Side of Front

Work even means to continue to work in the pattern as established, without working any increases or decreases.

Following Size in Patterns

The patterns for garments include a variety of sizes. Each pattern is written for the smallest size pattern with changes in the number of stitches (or inches) for other sizes in parentheses. For example, the pattern will tell you how many stitches to cast on as follows:

Cast on 20 (23, 24) stitches.

You would cast on 20 stitches for the small size, 23 stitches for the medium size and 24 stitches for the large size. Depending on the pattern there may be more sizes or fewer sizes given. Check the measurements to determine the best size to make.

Before you begin knitting, it might be helpful to highlight or circle all the numbers for the size you are making throughout the pattern.

Lesson 12

Finishing

Many a well-knitted garment, worked exactly to gauge, ends up looking sloppy and amateurish, simply because of bad finishing. Finishing a knitted garment requires no special skill, but it does require time, attention and knowledge of basic techniques.

Picking up Stitches

You will often need to pick up a certain number of stitches along an edge, such as around a sweater neckline or armhole, so that ribbing or an edging can be worked. The pattern instructions will usually clearly state where and how many stitches to pick up. Although this is not difficult, it is often done incorrectly, and the results look messy. Many times a circular needle is used for picking up stitches. For a neck edge, once the stitches are picked up, you begin knitting again in the first stitch and continue to work around the needle until the desired length is achieved.

To pick up a stitch, hold the knitting with the right side of the work facing you. Hold yarn from the skein behind the work, and hold a knitting needle in your right hand. Insert the point of the needle into the work from front to back, one stitch (at least two threads) from the edge; wrap the yarn around the needle as if knitting and draw the yarn through with the needle to the right side of the work making one stitch on the needle.

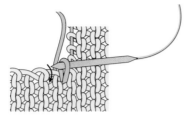

Pick up another stitch in the same manner, spacing stitches evenly along the edge.

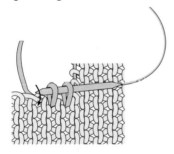

When picking up, pick up one stitch for each stitch when working across stitches in a horizontal row, and pick up about three stitches for every four rows when working along ends of rows. If a large number of stitches are to be picked up, it is best to mark off the edge into equal sections, then pick up the same number of stitches in each section.

For stitches that have been bound off along a neck edge, pick up through both loops of each stitch.

Sometimes stitches are placed on a holder when working the front and back of a garment. When picking up these stitches they can either be knit directly from the holder or slipped to another needle and knit from it, depending on how they were originally slipped onto the holder.

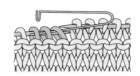

Blocking

Blocking simply means "setting" each piece into its final size and shape. (*Note: Be sure to check the yarn label before blocking, as some synthetic yarns and mohair yarns are ruined if they are blocked.*)

To block, moisten each piece first by dampening it with a light water spray. Then place each piece out on a padded flat surface (terry towelling provides adequate padding) right side up and away from direct sunlight. Referring to the small drawing or schematic in the pattern for the measurements for each piece, smooth out each piece to correct size and shape, using your fingers and the palms of your hands. Be sure to keep the stitches and rows in straight alignment. Use rust-proof straight pins to hold the edges in place. Let pieces dry completely before removing.

If further blocking is required, use steam from a steam iron. Hold the iron close to the knitted piece and allow the steam to penetrate the fabric. Never rest the iron directly on the piece—knitting should never have a pressed flat look. Let dry completely before removing.

Important Note: Never press ribbing, garter stitch, cables, or textured patterns as in Irish knits.

Sewing Seams

Your pattern will usually tell you in what order to assemble the pieces. Use the same yarn as used in the garment to sew the seams, unless the yarn is too thick, in which case, use a thinner yarn in a matching colour.

Invisible Seam

This seam gives a smooth and neat appearance, as it weaves the edges together invisibly from the right side.

To join horizontal edges, such as shoulder seams, sew the edges together as shown.

To join a front/back vertical edge to a horizontal sleeve edge, weave the edges together as shown.

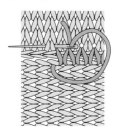

To join vertical edges, such as side seams or underarm sleeve seams, sew the edges together on the right side, pulling yarn gently until the edges meet.

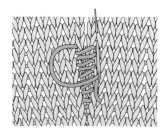

For pieces made using garter stitch, join vertical edges as shown.

Hint: When seaming, do not draw the stitches too tight, as the joining should have the same stretch or give as in the knitted garment.

Kitchener Stitch

This method of weaving with two needles is used for the toes of socks and flat seams. To weave the edges together and form an unbroken line of stockinette stitch, divide all stitches evenly onto two knitting needles—one behind the other. Thread yarn into tapestry needle. Hold needles with wrong sides together and work from right to left as follows:

1. Insert tapestry needle into first stitch on front needle as to purl. Draw yarn through stitch, leaving stitch on knitting needle.

2. Insert tapestry needle into the first stitch on the back needle as to purl. Draw yarn through stitch and slip stitch off knitting needle.

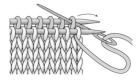

3. Insert tapestry needle into the next stitch on same (back) needle as to knit, leaving stitch on knitting needle.

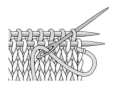

4. Insert tapestry needle into the first stitch on the front needle as to knit. Draw yarn through stitch and slip stitch off knitting needle.

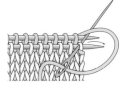

5. Insert tapestry needle into the next stitch on same (front) needle as to purl. Draw yarn through stitch, leaving stitch on knitting needle.

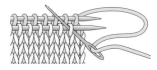

Repeat Steps 2 through 5 until one stitch is left on each needle. Then repeat Steps 2 and 4. Fasten off. Woven stitches should be the same size as adjacent knitted stitches.

Weaving in Ends

The final step is to weave in all the yarn ends securely. To do this, use a size 16 tapestry needle and weave the yarn end through the backs of stitches.

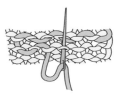

First weave the yarn about 2 inches in one direction and then 1 inch in the reverse direction. Cut off excess yarn.

If the ends are close to a seam weave the yarn back and forth along the edge of the seam.

Lesson 13

Substituting Yarn

When substituting a different yarn, you should stitch a swatch with the needle/hook size listed to make sure the yarn you have selected matches the gauge given in the pattern.

Changing Needle Size

If you need to stitch *more* stitches in your swatch to create the gauge listed, try the next size *smaller* needle/hook to see if this will give you the correct gauge.

If you need to stitch *fewer* stitches in your swatch to create the gauge listed, try the next size *larger* needle/hook to see if this will give you the gauge.

DETERMINE AMOUNT OF YARN NEEDED		
General conversion amounts for yarns given generically. *Yardages are approximations.*		
Lace (lace) weight:	1 ounce =	133 yards
Super fine (sock, fingering, baby) weight:	1 ounce =	170–175 yards
Fine (sport) weight:	1 ounce =	90–100 yards
Light (light worsted) weight:	1 ounce =	70–75 yards
Medium (worsted) weight:	1 ounce =	50 yards
Bulky (chunky) weight:	1 ounce =	30–35 yards
Super bulky (super chunky) weight:	1 ounce =	16–23 yards

Lesson 14

Special Techniques
Here are some intermediate techniques for casting on and binding off. Try these once you are proficient in the basic techniques.

Provisional Cast-On
The provisional cast-on has a variety of uses. It starts with a crochet chain on a crochet hook about the same size as the knitting needle. A chart is given below of crochet hooks that correspond most closely to knitting needle sizes.

Crochet Hook	Knitting Needle
E	4
F	5
G	6
H	8
I	9
J	10
K	10½

To work this type of cast-on, start with a crochet chain one or two stitches more than the number of stitches to be cast on for the pattern you are working. If the edge is to be decorative or removed to work in the opposite direction, then the chain should be made with a contrasting colour.

Once the chain is completed, with a knitting needle, pick up and knit in the back bump of each chain (Photo 1) until the required number of stitches is on the needle. Continue to work the pattern as given in the instructions.

Photo 1

Some instructions indicate that the provisional cast-on be removed so the piece can be worked in the opposite direction. In this case, hold the work with the cast-on edge at the top. Undo one loop of the crochet chain, inserting the knitting needle into the stitch below the chain. (This stitch is on the original first row of knitting). Continue to undo the crochet chain until all the stitches are on the needle. (Photo 2) This provides a row of stitches ready to work in the opposite direction.

Photo 2

3-Needle Bind-Off
Use this technique for seaming two edges together, such as when joining a shoulder seam. Hold the edge stitches on two separate needles with right sides together.

With a third needle, knit together a stitch from the front needle with one from the back.

Repeat, knitting a stitch from the front needle with one from the back needle once more.

Slip the first stitch over the second.

Repeat knitting, a front and back pair of stitches together, then bind one off.

Standard Abbreviations

[ ] work instructions within brackets as many times as directed

( ) work instructions within parentheses in the place directed

** repeat instructions following the asterisks as directed

* repeat instructions following the single asterisk as directed

" inch(es)

beg begin/beginning
CC contrasting colour
ch chain stitch
cm centimetre(s)
cn cable needle
dec decrease/decreases/ decreasing

dpn(s) double-pointed needle(s)
g gram
inc increase/increases/increasing
k knit
k2tog knit 2 stitches together
LH left hand
lp(s) loop(s)
m metre(s)
M1 make one stitch
MC main colour
mm millimetre(s)
oz ounce(s)
p purl
pat(s) pattern(s)
p2tog purl 2 stitches together
pm place marker

psso pass slipped stitch over
p2sso pass 2 slipped stitches over
rem remain/remaining
rep repeat(s)
rev St st reverse stockinette stitch
RH right hand
rnd(s) round(s)
RS right side
skp slip, knit, pass stitch over— one stitch decreased
sk2p slip 1, knit 2 together, pass slip stitch over the knit 2 together—2 stitches have been decreased
sl slip

sl 1k slip 1 knitwise
sl 1p slip 1 purlwise
sl st slip stitch(es)
ssk slip, slip, knit these 2 stitches together—a decrease
st(s) stitch(es)
St st stockinette stitch/ stocking stitch
tbl through back loop(s)
tog together
WS wrong side
wyib with yarn in back
wyif with yarn in front
yd(s) yard(s)
yfwd yarn forward
yo yarn over

Standard Yarn Weight System

Categories of yarn, gauge ranges, and recommended needle sizes

Yarn Weight Symbol & Category Names	1 SUPER FINE	2 FINE	3 LIGHT	4 MEDIUM	5 BULKY	6 SUPER BULKY
Type of Yarns in Category	Sock, Fingering, Baby	Sport, Baby	DK, Light Worsted	Worsted, Afghan, Aran	Chunky, Craft, Rug	Bulky, Roving
Knit Gauge* Ranges in Stockinette Stitch to 4 inches	21–32 sts	23–26 sts	21–24 sts	16–20 sts	12–15 sts	6–11 sts
Recommended Needle in Metric Size Range	2.25– 3.25mm	3.25– 3.75mm	3.75– 4.5mm	4.5– 5.5mm	5.5–8mm	8mm
Recommended Needle Canada/U.S. Size Range	1 to 3	3 to 5	5 to 7	7 to 9	9 to 11	11 and larger

* GUIDELINES ONLY: The above reflect the most commonly used gauges and needle sizes for specific yarn categories.

Sweet Dreams Blanket

This crib-size blanket is soft as a cloud.

Design | Cindy Adams

Skill Level

EASY

Finished Measurements
Approx 32 x 48 inches

Materials
Bulky weight bouclé acrylic yarn (180 yds/100g
   per ball): 3 balls antique white
Size 10 (6mm) needles or size needed to obtain gauge

Gauge
10 sts = 4 inches/10cm in pat
To save time, take time to check gauge.

Pattern Note
On all rows, knit first st tbl; sl last st wyif.

Blanket
Cast on 74 sts, knit 8 rows for border, working edge sts as above.

Body
Row 1 (RS): K1-tbl, knit to last st, end sl 1 wyif.

Row 2: K1-tbl, k4, *p4, yo; rep from * to last 5 sts, end k4, sl 1 wyif.

Row 3: K1-tbl, k4, *drop yo from previous row, yo, sl 1, k3, pass sl st over 3 knit sts; rep from * to last 5 sts, end k4, sl 1 wyif.

Row 4: K5, purl to last 5 sts, end k4, sl 1 wyif.

Rep Rows 1–4 until blanket measures approx 46 inches from beg.

Border
Knit 8 rows, bind off all sts. ■

Sweet Dreams Blanket
Sample project was knit with
Baby Bouclé (97 per cent acrylic/
3 per cent polyester) from Bernat.

RAINBOW BLANKET

The stripes blaze a bright trail for any nursery scheme, and knit up with an easy lace design.

Design | Patsy Leatherbury

Skill Level
EASY

Finished Measurements
Approx 36½ x 40 inches

Materials
DK weight mercerized cotton/acrylic blend yarn
(136 yds/50g per ball): 2 balls each lavender
(A), light purple (B), blue (C), turquoise (D),
green (E), lime (F), yellow (G), orange (H), coral (I)
Size 7 (4.5mm) needles or size needed to obtain gauge

Gauge
18 sts and 27 rows = 4 inches/10cm in pat
To save time, take time to check gauge.

Blanket
With A, cast on 165 sts.

Lower border
Rows 1–12: Knit every row.

Row 13: Knit across.

Row 14: K10, purl to last 10 sts, k10.

Body
Row 1 (RS): Knit across.

Rows 2, 4, 6, 8 and 10: K10, purl to last 10 sts, k10.

Row 3: K14, *k2tog, yo, k1, yo, ssk, k7; rep from * to last 19 sts, k2tog, yo, k1, yo, ssk, k14.

Rows 5 and 7: Knit across.

Row 9: K20, *k2tog, yo, k1, yo, ssk, k7; rep from * to last 25 sts, k2tog, yo, k1, yo, ssk, k20.

Row 11: Knit.

Row 12: K10, purl to last 10 sts, k10.

Rows 13–18: [Rep Rows 1–6] once more. Cut A.

Rows 19–48: Attach B, work [Rows 7–12] once, then [Rows 1–12] twice. Cut B.

Rows 49–78: Attach C, work [Rows 1–12] twice, then [Rows 1–6] once. Cut C.

Rows 79–108: Attach D, work [Rows 7–12] once, then [Rows 1–12] twice. Cut D.

Rows 109–138: Attach E, work [Rows 1–12] twice, then [Rows 1–6] once. Cut E.

Rainbow Blanket
Sample project was knit with Wildflower DK (51 per cent mercerized cotton/49 per cent acrylic) from Plymouth Yarn Co.

Rows 139–168: Attach F, work [Rows 7–12] once, then [Rows 1–12] twice. Cut F.

Rows 169–198: Attach G, work [Rows 1–12] twice, then [Rows 1–6] once. Cut G.

Rows 199–228: Attach H, work [Rows 7–12] once, then [Rows 1–12] twice. Cut H.

Rows 229–246: Attach I, work [Rows 1–12] once, then [Rows 1–6] once. Do not cut I.

Upper border
Rows 1–12: With I, knit every row.

Bind off knitwise. ■

PATCHWORK CHECKS

Bows or chicks combined with checks are fun to stitch while waiting for Baby to arrive.

Designs | Scarlet Taylor

Skill Level

INTERMEDIATE

Finished Measurements
Approx 30 x 30 inches

Gauge
Gingham square: 28 sts and 30 rows = 5 inches/12.5cm square with larger needles
Solid square: 28 sts and 38 rows = 5 inches/12/5cm square with smaller needles in St st
Bow or chick square: 27 sts and 38 rows = 5 inches/12.5cm square with smaller needles in St st
To save time, take time to check gauge.

Pattern Notes
When working Gingham Square, carry colour not in use loosely across back.
For more information on changing colours to work bow or chick, see page 19.

Girl's Afghan

Materials
Light weight acrylic yarn (468 yds/5 oz per ball): 1 ball each white (A) and pink (B), 2 balls pink (C)
Size 6 (4mm) straight and 24-inch circular needles or size needed to obtain gauge
Size 7 (4.5mm) needles or size needed to obtain gauge

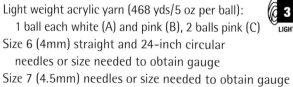

Gingham Square
Make 10

With larger needles and C, cast on 28 sts.

Row 1 (RS): K3 B, *k2 C, k2 B; rep from * to last st, k1 B.

Row 2: P3 B, *p2 C, p2 B; rep from * to last st, p1 B.

Row 3: K3 A, *k2 B, k2 A; rep from * to last st, k1 A.

Row 4: P3 A, *p2 B, p2 A; rep from * to last st, p1 A.

Rows 5–28: [Rep Rows 1–4] 6 times.

Rows 29 and 30: Rep Rows 1 and 2.

Bind off all sts with C.

Solid Square
Make 14

With smaller needles and C, cast on 28 sts. Work in St st until block measures 5 inches, ending with a WS row.

Bind off all sts.

Patchwork Checks
Sample projects were knit with Softee Baby (100 per cent acrylic) from Bernat.

Bow Square
Make 12

With smaller needles and A, cast on 27 sts.

Rows 1 and 2: Beg with a RS row, work 2 rows in St st.

Row 3 (RS): Join C, k1 C, *k1 A, k1 C; rep from * across.

Row 4: P1 A, *p1 C, p1 A; rep from * across.

Rows 5–14: Cut C, and work 10 rows in St st with A.

Row 15 (RS): K9, place marker, work Row 1 of Bow Chart over next 9 sts, place marker, work to end.

Rows 16–24: Continue as established, working pat from chart between markers until Row 10 has been completed.

Rows 25–34: Removing markers, continue in St st and A only for 10 rows more.

Row 35 (RS): Join C, k1 C, *k1 A, k1 C; rep from * across.

Row 36: P1 A, *p1 C, p1 A; rep from * across.

Rows 37 and 38: Cut C, and work 2 rows St st with A.

Bind off all sts.

Assembly
Referring to Assembly Diagram on next page for placement of squares, sew 6 rows of 6 squares each tog.

Border
With smaller circular needle and A, pick up and knit 126 sts evenly across 1 edge of afghan. Do not join; work back and forth in garter st, inc 1 st at each end of needle every other row until border measures approx 1 inch. Bind off loosely.

Rep for rem 3 sides of afghan. Seam mitred corners.

Boy's Afghan

Materials
Light weight acrylic yarn (468 yds/5 oz per ball):
   1 ball each white (A), pale blue, (B) lemon (D) and 2 balls blue (C)
Size 6 (4mm) straight and 24-inch circular needles or size needed to obtain gauge
Size 7 (4.5mm) needles or size needed to obtain gauge
Small amount black embroidery floss or yarn

Gingham Square
Make 10 as for Girl's Afghan.

Solid Square
Make 14 as for Girl's Afghan.

Chick Square
Make 12

With smaller needles and B, cast on 27 sts. Beg with a RS row, work 14 rows in St st.

Next row (RS): Knit 8 sts, place marker, work Row 1 of Chick Chart over next 11 sts, place marker, work to end.

Continue as established, working pat from chart between markers until Row 10 has been completed.

Removing markers, continue in St st and B only for 14 rows more. Bind off all sts.

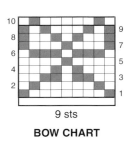

9 sts

BOW CHART

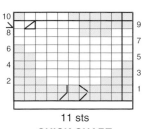

11 sts

CHICK CHART

Assembly

Work embroidery on chicks as shown on chart.

Referring to Assembly Diagram for placement of squares, sew 6 rows of 6 squares each tog.

Border

With smaller circular needle and C, RS facing, pick up and knit 142 sts along 1 edge of afghan. Do not join. Work in k2, p2 rib, inc 1 st at each side [every row] 8 times. Bind off in rib.

Rep for rem 3 sides of afghan. Seam mitred corners. ■

1	2	3	1	2	3
2	3	1	2	3	1
3	1	2	3	1	2
1	2	3	1	2	3
2	3	1	2	3	1
3	1	2	3	1	2

Assembly Diagram

1. Gingham Square
2. Solid Square
3. Chick or Bow Square

JUST DUCKY BLANKIE

Here's the perfect baby gift for the next dear little duckling to arrive!

Design | Patsy Leatherbury

Skill Level

BEGINNER

Finished Measurements

Approx 42 x 48 inches

Materials

Bulky weight nylon yarn (90 yds/50g per ball): 10 balls baby mix (A)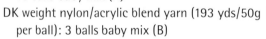

DK weight nylon/acrylic blend yarn (193 yds/50g per ball): 3 balls baby mix (B)

Size 10 (6mm) needles or size needed to obtain gauge

4½-inch square yellow fleece (for duck appliqué)

4 inches ⅛-inch-wide ribbon

Ready-made rosette or bow

Embroidery needle and yellow embroidery floss to match fleece

Gauge

10 sts and 17 rows = 4 inches/10cm in Seed st

To save time, take time to check gauge.

Afghan

With A, cast on 109 sts.

Row 1: K1, *p1, k1; rep from * across.

Rep Row 1 until piece measures 48 inches.

Bind off in pat.

Fringe

Cut 9-inch lengths of B. Referring to page 26, make Single Knot Fringe. Use 4 strands for each knot, placing knots on all 4 sides of afghan.

Duck Appliqué

Referring to drawing, cut duck shape from fleece. Use B to stem stitch wing outline as in photo. Make French knot for eye of duck. Sew ribbon to neck of duck. With embroidery floss, work blanket stitch around outer edge. Sew as desired in lower left corner of blanket. Sew rosette to neck. ■

Stem Stitch

Bring yarn up along imaginary line for wing. Keeping yarn consistently either below or above the needle, take a stitch as shown. Continue in this manner to form wing.

Stem Stitch

A little something...

Just Ducky Blankie
Sample project was knit with Plush Colors (100 per cent nylon) from Berroco and Cuddly Classic DK (55 per cent nylon/ 45 per cent acrylic) from Euro Yarns.

French Knot

Bring yarn from wrong to right side. Wrap once around shaft of needle. Insert needle into loop. Pull wrapping yarn snug around needle and hold as needle is pulled to wrong side.

French Knot

Blanket Stitch

This stitch is worked along edge of piece. Bring needle up and make a counterclockwise lp. Take stitch as indicated, keeping the thread beneath the point of needle. Pull through to form stitch. Continue in same manner around outer edge.

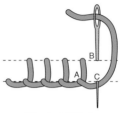

Blanket Stitch

Just Ducky

BUNDLES OF JOY

Make this while you wait for a new arrival, and be ready to wrap your new bundle with love!

Design | Kathy Wesley

Skill Level

EASY

Finished Measurements

Approx 36 x 42 inches (excluding fringe)

Materials

DK weight nylon/acrylic blend yarn (185 yds/50g per ball): 8 balls blue and 3 balls white

3 LIGHT

Size 6 (4mm) 36-inch circular needle or size needed to obtain gauge

Gauge

20 sts = 4 inches/10cm in St st
To save time, take time to check gauge.

Pattern Notes

Colour not in use is carried along edge of afghan. When carrying the old colour along edge, bring the working colour under the old colour at the beg of the row, to lock it in place.

When changing to a new colour at the beg of the row, bring the new colour under the old colour.

Sl all sts as if to purl.

Afghan

With blue, cast on 185 sts.

Row 1 (RS): Knit.

Row 2: Purl. Drop blue.

Row 3: With white, k4, *sl 3 wyif, k3 wyib; rep from * to last st, end k1.

Row 4: P4, *sl 3 wyib, p3 wyif; rep from * to last st, end p1. Drop white.

Row 5: With blue, knit.

Row 6: Purl.

Row 7: K5, *insert RH needle under 2 strands of white and into next st on LH needle as if to knit, knit st and bring strands over needle, k5; rep from * across.

Row 8: Purl. Drop blue.

Row 9: With white, k1, *sl 3 wyif, k3 wyib; rep from * to last 4 sts, end sl 3 wyif, k1 wyib.

Row 10: P1, *sl 3 wyib, p3 wyif; rep from * to last 4 sts, end sl 3 wyib, p1 wyif. Drop white.

Row 11: With blue, knit.

Row 12: Purl.

Row 13: K1, *insert RH needle under 2 strands of white and into next st on LH needle, knit st and bring strands over needle, k5; rep from * to last 3 sts, insert RH needle under 2 strands of white and into next st on LH needle, knit st and bring strands over needle, k2.

Row 14: Purl. Drop blue.

Rows 15–362: [Rep Rows 3–14] until piece measures approx 42 inches ending with Row 7.

Fringe

Make Single Knot fringe referring to information at right. Cut 20-inch lengths of blue yarn; use 6 strands for each knot. Tie knots evenly spaced (about every ½ inch) across cast-on edge of afghan.

Fringe only cast-on edge of afghan, to avoid having fringe close to baby's face. ■

Fringe

Cut a piece of cardboard half as long as specified in instructions for length of strands plus ½ inch for trimming. Wind yarn loosely and evenly around cardboard. When cardboard is filled, cut yarn across one end. Do this several times, then begin fringing. Wind additional strands as necessary.

Single-Knot Fringe

Hold specified number of strands for one knot together, fold in half. Hold project to be fringed with right side facing you. Use crochet hook to draw folded end through space or stitch indicated from right to wrong side.

Pull loose ends through folded section.

Draw knot up firmly. Space knots as indicated in pattern instructions.

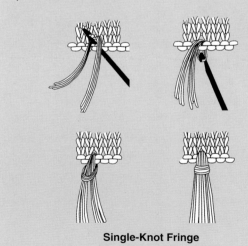

Single-Knot Fringe

Bundles of Joy
Sample project was knit with Angel Baby DK (55 per cent nylon/45 per cent acrylic) from S.R. Kertzer.

BABY BASKET BEANIE & BLANKIE

When you need a baby gift in a hurry, try this simple basket-weave stitch set. Choose either a solid or multicoloured yarn for impressive results.

Designs | Nazanin Fard

Skill Level

EASY

Size
Newborn

Finished Measurement
Blanket
30 x 30 inches
Hat
Circumference: 9¾ inches

Materials
Worsted weight yarn (197 yds/100g per ball):
  5 balls cream #607
Size 7 (4.5 mm) 24-inch (or longer) circular needle (for blanket) or size needed to obtain gauge
Size 7 (4.5 mm) set of 4 double-pointed needles (for hat) or size needed to obtain gauge
Stitch markers
Tapestry needle

Gauge
22 sts and 32 rows = 4 inches/10cm in pat
To save time, take time to check gauge.

Pattern Note
Always sl sts purlwise, holding yarn to WS.

Pattern Stitches
A. Basket Weave (multiple of 6 sts + 8)

Row 1 (RS): Knit.

Row 2: K4, purl to last 4 sts, k4.

Rows 3 and 5: K4, *sl 2, k4; rep from * to last 4 sts, k4.

Rows 4 and 6: K4, *k4, sl 2; rep from * to end.

Row 7: Knit.

Row 8: Rep Row 2.

Rows 9 and 11: K4, *k3, sl 2, k1; rep from * to last 4 sts, k4.

Rows 10 and 12: K4, *k1, sl 2, k3; rep from * to last 4 sts, k4.

Rep Rows 1–12 for pat.

B. Basket Weave (in the round) (multiple of 6 sts)

Rnds 1 and 2: Knit.

Rnds 3 and 5: *Sl 2, k4; rep from * around.

Rnds 4 and 6: *Sl 2, p4; rep from * around.

Baby Basket Beanie & Blankie
Sample projects were knit with classic worsted (80 per cent acrylic/20 per cent wool) from Universal Yarn Inc.

Rnds 7 and 8: Knit.

Rnds 9 and 11: *K3, sl 2, k1; rep from * around.

Rnds 10 and 12: *P3, sl 2, p1; rep from * around.

Rep Rnds 1–12 for pat.

Blanket

Pattern Notes
Pat is worked back and forth; a circular needle is used
    to accommodate the large number of sts.
Sl sts purlwise with yarn to WS.

Instructions
Cast on 158 sts.

Knit 6 rows.

Work even in Basket Weave pat until piece measures
29 inches.

Knit 6 rows.

Bind off all sts loosely.

Block blanket to size.

Hat

Border
Cast on 54 sts.

Distribute evenly on 3 dpns, place marker for beg of rnd
and join, making sure not to twist sts.

Work 10 rnds of k1, p1 rib.

Body
Work 3 reps of 12-rnd Basket Weave (in the round) pat,
then work Rnds 1 and 2 again.

Shape crown
Rnd 1: *K4, k2tog; rep from * around. (45 sts)

Rnd 2: Knit.

Rnd 3: *K3, k2tog; rep from * around. (36 sts)

Rnds 4 and 5: Knit.

Rnd 6: K2tog around. (18 sts)

Rnd 7: Knit.

Rnd 8: Rep Rnd 6. (9 sts)

Rnd 9: *K1, k2tog; rep from * around. (6 sts)

Rnd 10: Rep Rnd 6. (3 sts)

I-Cord
Sl all 3 sts to 1 needle. *K3, do not turn, sl sts back to LH needle; rep from * for 10 rows.

Bind off.

Cut yarn, leaving a 6-inch tail.

Finishing
Weave in all ends.

With a tapestry needle, sew the end of I-cord to the top of hat. ■

SHOWER BABY WITH GIFTS

Welcome a newborn with knitted niceties that are new-mom pleasers!

Designs | Patsy Leatherbury

Blanket

Skill Level

EASY

Finished Measurements
Approx 32 x 34 inches

Materials
DK weight acrylic yarn (262 yds/100g per ball):
  2 balls each yellow and aqua, 1 ball white
Size 6 (4mm) needles or size needed to obtain gauge

Gauge
18 sts and 26 rows = 4 inches/10cm in St st
To save time, take time to check gauge.

Blanket
With aqua, cast on 141 sts.

Knit 12 rows.

Beg pat
Row 1: Knit.

Rows 2, 4, 6, 8 and 10: K10, purl to last 10 sts, k10.

Row 3: K14, yo, ssk, k1, k2tog, yo, *k7, yo, ssk, k1, k2tog, yo; rep from * to last 14 sts, end k14.

Row 5: K15, yo, sl 1, k2tog, psso, yo, *k9, yo, sl 1, k2tog, psso, yo; rep from * to last 15 sts, end k15.

Row 7: Knit.

Row 9: K20, *yo, ssk, k1, k2tog, yo, k7; rep from * to last 13 sts, end k13.

Row 11: K21, *yo, sl 1, k2tog, psso, yo, k9; rep from * to last 12 sts, end k12.

Row 12: K10, purl to last 10 sts, k10.

Rows 13–30: Change to yellow, work Rows 1–12 once, then rep Rows 1–6 once.

Rows 31–48: Change to aqua, work Rows 7–12 once, then rep Rows 1–12 once.

Rows 49–72: Change to white, work Rows 1–12 twice.

Rows 73–90: Change to aqua, work Rows 1–12 once, then rep Rows 1–6 once.

Rows 91–120: Change to yellow, work Rows 7–12 once, then rep Rows 1–12 twice.

Rows 121–138: Change to aqua, work Rows 1–12 once, then rep Rows 1–6 once.

Shower Baby With Gifts
Sample projects were knit with Sirdar
Tropicana Cotton Effect DK (100 per
cent acrylic) from Knitting Fever Inc.

Rows 139–162: Change to white, work Rows 7–12 once, Rows 1–12 once, then Rows 1–6 once.

Rows 163–180: Change to aqua, work Rows 7–12 once, then rep Rows 1–12 once.

Rows 181–198: Change to yellow, work Rows 1–12 once, then rep Rows 1–6 once.

Rows 199–210: Change to aqua, work Rows 7–12 once, then rep Rows 1–6 once.

Rows 211–222: Knit every row.

Bind off all sts.

Cap

Skill Level
INTERMEDIATE

Sizes
Infant 0–3 (6–12) months. Instructions are given for smaller size, with larger size in parentheses. When only 1 number is given, it applies to both sizes.

Finished Measurement
Circumference: approx 14 (14½) inches

Materials
DK weight acrylic yarn (262 yds/100g per ball): 1 ball each yellow, aqua and white
Size 4 (3.5mm) circular needle
Size 6 (4mm) circular and double-pointed needles or size needed to obtain gauge
Stitch marker

3 LIGHT

Gauge
18 sts and 26 rnds = 4 inches/10cm in St st
To save time, take time to check gauge.

Pattern Stitch
K1, P1 Rib (even number of sts)

Rnd 1: *K1, p1; rep from * around.

Rep Rnd 1 for pat.

Cap

Border
With smaller circular needle and white, cast on 72 (84) sts; mark beg of rnd, and join without twisting. Work 2 rnds K1, P1 Rib.

Change to aqua. Work 13 (17) rnds K1, P1 Rib.

Change to larger circular needle and knit 6 rnds.

Body
Beg pat
Rnds 1 and 2: Knit around.

Rnd 3: K3, *yo, ssk, k1, k2tog, yo, k7; rep from * to last 9 sts, end yo, ssk, k1, k2tog, yo, k4.

Rnd 4: Knit around.

Rnd 5: K4, *yo, sl 1, k2tog, psso, yo, k9; rep from * to last 8 sts, end yo, sl 1, k2tog, psso, yo, k5.

Rnd 6: Knit around.

Rnds 7, 8 and 10: Change to yellow, knit around.

Rnd 9: K2tog, yo, k7, *yo, ssk, k1, k2tog, yo, k7; rep from * to last 3 sts, end yo, ssk, k1.

Rnd 11: K1, yo, k9, *yo, sl 1, k2tog, psso, yo, k9; rep from * to last 2 sts, end sl 1, knit last st of this rnd and first st of next rnd tog (remove marker), psso, replace rnd marker after st is worked.

Rnd 12: Knit around.

Knit 2 (10) rnds. Work rem of cap in St st (knit every rnd).

Shape crown
Note: Work may be transferred to dpns as needed.

First dec rnd for size 6–12 months only: *K2tog, k5; rep from * around. (72 sts)

Size 6–12 months only: Knit 5 rnds even.

Both sizes
Rnd 1: *K2tog, k4; rep from * around. (60 sts)

Rnds 2–5: Knit 4 rnds even.

Rnd 6: *K2tog, k3; rep from * around. (48 sts)

Rnds 7–9: Knit 3 rnds even.

Rnd 10: *K2tog, k2; rep from * around. (36 sts)

Rnds 11 and 12: Knit 2 rnds even.

Rnd 13: *K2tog, k1; rep from * around. (24 sts)

Rnd 14: Knit 1 rnd even.

Rnd 15: [K2tog] around. (12 sts)

Cut yarn, leaving a 6-inch end. Draw tail through rem sts, pull tight and fasten off.

Bottle Cozy

Skill Level
EASY

Finished Measurement
To fit average 8-oz bottle

Materials
DK weight yarn (262 yds/100g per ball): 1 ball each yellow, aqua and white
Size 6 (4mm) needles or size needed to obtain gauge
Stitch marker
¼-inch satin ribbon: 24 inches

Gauge
18 sts and 26 rows = 4 inches/10cm
To save time, take time to check gauge.

Bottle Cozy
With white, cast on 25 sts.

Row 1: Knit across.

Row 2: [P1, (k1, p1) in next st] 12 times, p1. (37 sts)

Row 3: Knit.

Row 4: Purl.

Row 5: *K1, p1; rep from * to last st, end k1.

Row 6: *P1, k1; rep from* to last st, end p1.

Rows 7–12: [Rep Rows 5 and 6] 6 times.

Rows 13–16: Change to aqua, knit every row.

Beg pat
Row 1: Change to white, knit across.

Rows 2, 4 and 6: Purl.

Row 3: K4, yo, ssk, k1, k2tog, yo, *k7, yo, ssk, k1, k2tog, yo; rep from * to last 4 sts, end k4.

Row 5: K5, yo, sl 1, k2tog, psso, yo, *k9, yo, sl 1, k2tog, psso, yo; rep from * to last 5 sts, end k5.

Row 7: Knit.

Row 8: Purl.

Rows 9–20: Change to yellow, knit every row.

Rows 21–28: Change to white, rep Rows 1–8 of pat.

Rows 29–32: Change to aqua, knit every row.

Row 33: Change to white, *k1, p1; rep from * to last st, end k1.

Row 34: *P1, k1; rep from * to last st, end p1.

Rows 35 and 36: Rep Rows 33 and 34.

Row 37 (eyelet row): *K2tog, yo; rep from * to last st, end k1.

Row 38: Purl.

Rows 39–42: Knit every row.

Change to aqua, and bind off all sts.

Assembly
Sew back seam.

Thread a piece of white yarn through cast-on sts at bottom of piece, draw tight and fasten off. Run ribbon through eyelets, fit snug on bottle and tie ribbon in a bow.

Pacifier Holder

Materials

DK weight acrylic yarn (262 yds/100q per ball):
    Small amounts each yellow, aqua and white
Size 6 (4mm) needles or size needed to obtain gauge
Small jaw hair clip
¼-inch satin ribbon: 10 inches yellow
Small amount batting or stuffing
2 small ribbon flowers
Small snap set
Glue

Gauge

18 sts and 26 rows = 4 inches/10cm in St st
To save time, take time to check gauge.

Pacifier Holder

With white, cast on 6 sts, leaving a 6-inch tail at free end
of yarn.

Row 1 (RS): Knit across.

Row 2: Change to yellow, [k1, p1] in each st across. (12 sts)

Row 3: Knit.

Row 4: Rep Row 2. (24 sts)

Row 5: Knit.

Row 6: Purl.

Row 7: Change to aqua, knit across.

Row 8: Change to yellow, purl across.

Row 9: Knit.

Row 10: Change to aqua, purl across.

Row 11: Change to yellow, knit across.

Row 12: Purl.

Row 13: Knit.

Row 14: [P2tog] across. (12 sts)

Row 15: Knit.

Row 16: [P2tog] across. (6 sts)

Bind off all sts.

Small Fins
Make 2

With yellow, cast on 5 sts.

Row 1: Knit.

Row 2: P2tog, p1, p2tog. (3 sts)

Row 3: Sl 1, k2tog, psso. (1 st)

Cut yarn, pull tail through rem lp and fasten off.

Large Fin
With white, cast on 10 sts.

Rows 1 and 3: Knit.

Row 2: K2tog, k6, k2tog. (8 sts)

Row 4: K2tog, k4, k2tog. (6 sts)

Bind off rem sts.

Assembly

With beg tail of white yarn, run yarn through cast-on sts and pull snug to close opening. This is mouth of fish.

Holding RS tog, sew back seam of fish. Turn RS out.

Stuff batting through rem opening, shaping fish body into a slightly flattened ball. Sew rem opening closed.

Referring to photo, sew large fin to top of fish; sew 1 small fin to each side, and satin st with aqua yarn to make eyes.

Glue jaw hairclip to back of fish (for tail) with claw end of clip facing away from fish. Use a small amount of glue on each side of clip, so clip can open and close easily. Hold in place with rubber band while glue dries, if desired.

Fold 2½ inches of ribbon over with WS tog and sew in place. Place 1 side of snap set next to raw edge of ribbon and sew in place. Place other side of snap set next to fold of ribbon and sew in place. Sew ribbon flowers on ribbon on opposite sides of snap. Sew other end of ribbon to bottom of fish. Pull snap end of ribbon through pacifier handle and snap closed. Jaw clasp (fish tail) will serve as clamp to anchor pacifier.

Washcloths

Skill Level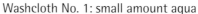
EASY

Finished Measurement
Approx 8½ inches square

Materials
DK weight acrylic yarn (262 yds/100g per ball):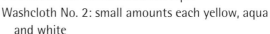
Washcloth No. 1: small amount aqua
Washcloth No. 2: small amounts each yellow, aqua and white
Washcloth No. 3: small amounts each yellow and white
Size 6 (4mm) needles or size needed to obtain gauge

Gauge
18 sts and 26 rows = 4 inches/10cm in St st
Exact gauge is not critical to this project.

Washcloth No. 1
With aqua, cast on 43 sts. Knit every row for 6 rows.

Beg pat
Row 1 (RS): Knit across.

Row 2 and all WS rows: K4, purl to last 4 sts, end k4.

Row 3: *K7, yo, ssk, k1, k2tog, yo; rep from * to last 7 sts, end k7.

Row 5: K8, yo, sl 1, k2tog, psso, yo, *k9, yo, sl 1, k2tog, psso, yo; rep from * to last 8 sts, end k8.

Row 7: Knit.

Row 9: K13, *yo, ssk, k1, k2tog, yo, k7; rep from * to last 6 sts, end k6.

Row 11: K14, *yo, sl 1, k2tog, psso, yo, k9; rep from * to last 5 sts, end k5.

Row 12: K4, purl to last 4 sts, k4.

Rows 13–44: Rep [Rows 1–12] twice, then [Rows 1–8] once more.

Knit every row for 6 rows. Bind off all sts.

Washcloth No. 2
With aqua, cast on 43 sts. Knit every row for 6 rows.

Beg pat
Row 1: Change to white, knit across.

Rows 2, 4 and 6: K4, purl to last 4 sts, end k4.

Row 3: *K7, yo, ssk, k1, k2tog, yo; rep from * to last 7 sts, end k7.

Row 5: K8, yo, sl 1, k2tog, psso, yo, *k9, yo, sl 1, k2tog, psso, yo; rep from * to last 8 sts, end k8.

Row 7: Knit.

Row 8: K4, purl to last 4 sts, k4.

Rows 9–26: Change to yellow, knit every row.

Rows 27 and 29: Change to aqua, knit across.

Rows 28, 30, 32 and 34: K4, purl to last 4 sts, k4.

Row 31: K13, *yo, ssk, k1, k2tog, yo, k7; rep from * to last 6 sts, end k6.

Row 33: K14, *yo, sl 1, k2tog, psso, yo, k9; rep from * to last 5 sts, end k5.

Row 35: Knit across.

Row 36: K4, purl to last 4 sts, end k4.

Rows 37–54: Change to yellow, knit every row.

Rows 55–62: Change to white, rep Rows 1–8.

Change to aqua, knit every row for 6 rows. Bind off all sts.

Washcloth No. 3
With yellow, cast on 43 sts.

Rows 1–12: Knit every row.

Rows 13–16: Change to white, knit every row.

Rows 17–28: Change to yellow, knit every row.

Rows 29–76: [Rep Rows 13–28] 3 times.

Bind off all sts. ■

ALPHABET BLOCKS

Block letters are featured on pastel squares to create an heirloom afghan, wall hanging and block for that special new baby.

Designs | Diane Zangl

Skill Level
EASY

Finished Measurements
Afghan: Approximately 37 x 41 inches
Wall Hanging: 15 x 15 inches
Block: 4 inches square

Materials
Worsted weight acrylic/wool blend yarn (200 yds/100g per ball): 6 balls natural (MC), 1 ball each aqua (A), fuchsia (B) and lime (C)
Size 6 (4mm) needles or size needed to obtain gauge
⅝-inch-wide flat wooden stick or dowel
Polyester fibrefill
Yarn needle

Gauge
18 sts and 27 rows = 4 inches/10cm in St st
To save time, take time to check gauge.

Pattern Stitch
Seed Pattern
Row 1 (RS): Sl 1 purlwise wyif, *p1, k1; rep from * across, end last rep p1.

Row 2: Sl 1 knitwise wyib, *k1, p1; rep from * across, end last rep k1.

Rep Rows 1 and 2 for pat.

Pattern Notes
Sl first st of every row for afghan and wall hanging.

Wind separate balls of colour for each section. To avoid holes when changing colours, always bring new colour up over old.

MC is used for Seed pat only; CC blocks are worked in St st. When working a Seed pat block above a CC one, always knit first row to avoid colour showing through.

Wall Hanging

With MC, cast on 64 sts. Sl first st of every row, work even in Seed pat for 7 rows.

First Tier of Blocks
Set up pat (RS): With MC, work Seed pat over 5 sts, k18 A, MC Seed pat over 18 sts, k18 B, MC Seed pat over 5 sts.

Keeping MC in Seed pat and colour blocks in St st, work even for 25 more rows.

Second Tier of Blocks
Set up pat (RS): Work Seed pat over 5 sts, k18 MC, k18 C, k18 MC, Seed pat over 5 sts.

Keeping MC in Seed pat and colour blocks in St st, work even for 25 more rows.

Alphabet Blocks
Sample projects were knit with
Encore (75 per cent acrylic/25 per cent
wool) from Plymouth Yarn Co.

Referring to charts, on page 54, duplicate st letters on each colour block.

Slide flat wooden stick into casing.

Block

Cast on 18 C, 18 B, 18 A.

Work even in St st for 25 more rows.

Next row (RS): Bind off 18 sts with A, cut B, attach MC, k18 MC, bind off 18 sts with C.

Working with MC on centre square only, [work in Seed pat for 25 rows, do not sl first st. Purl next RS row] twice.

Work in Seed pat for 25 rows.

Bind off all sts.

Third Tier of Blocks
Set up pat (RS): Work Seed pat over 5 sts, k18 B, k18 MC, k18 A, Seed pat over 5 sts.

Keeping MC in Seed pat and colour blocks in St st, work even for 25 more rows.

Work even in Seed pat only for 8 rows.

Facing
Purl next RS row for turning ridge. Work 7 rows in St st.

Bind off all sts.

Finishing
Turn facing to inside and sew in place.

Finishing
Referring to charts, duplicate st letters on each colour block.

Sew bound-off edge of lime square to side edge of first natural square.

Rep for aqua square.

Lightly stuff block with fibrefill.

Sew 3 sides of remaining natural squares to sides of aqua and lime and tops of all three coloured squares.

Afghan

With MC, cast on 156 sts. Work in Seed pat for 7 rows.

First Tier of Blocks
Set up pat (RS): Sl 1, work Seed pat over 5 sts, k18 C, Seed pat over 36 sts, k18 B, Seed pat over 36 sts, k18 A, Seed pat to end of row.

Keeping MC in Seed pat and colour blocks in St st, work even for 25 more rows.

Second Tier of Blocks
Set up pat (RS): Sl 1, Seed pat over 41 sts, k18 B, Seed pat over 36 sts, k18 A, Seed pat to end of row.

Keeping MC in Seed pat and colour blocks in St st, work even for 25 more rows.

Third Tier of Blocks
Set up pat (RS): Sl 1, Seed pat over 23 sts, k18 B, Seed pat over 36 sts, k18 A, Seed pat over 36 sts, k18 C, Seed pat to end of row.

Keeping MC in Seed pat and colour blocks in St st, work even for 25 more rows.

Fourth Tier of Blocks
Set up pat (RS): Sl 1, Seed pat over 5 sts, k18 B, Seed pat over 36 sts, k18 A, Seed pat over 36 sts, k18 C, Seed pat to end of row.

Keeping MC in Seed pat and colour blocks in St st, work even for 25 more rows.

Fifth Tier of Blocks
Set up pat (RS): Sl 1, Seed pat over 41 sts, k18 A, Seed pat over 36 sts, k18 C, Seed pat to end of row.

Keeping MC in Seed pat and colour blocks in St st, work even for 25 more rows.

Sixth Tier of Blocks
Set up pat (RS): Sl 1, Seed pat over 23 sts, k18 A, Seed pat over 36 sts, k18 C, Seed pat over 36 sts, k18 B, Seed pat to end of row.

Keeping MC in Seed pat and colour blocks in St st, work even for 25 more rows.

Seventh Tier of Blocks
Set up pat (RS): Sl 1, Seed pat over 5 sts, k18 A, Seed pat over 36 sts, k18 C, Seed pat over 36 sts, k18 B, Seed pat to end of row.

Keeping MC in Seed pat and colour blocks in St st, work even for 25 more rows.

Eighth Tier of Blocks

Set up pat (RS): Sl 1, Seed pat over 41 sts, k18 C, Seed pat over 36 sts, k18 B, Seed pat to end of row.

Keeping MC in Seed pat and colour blocks in St st, work even for 25 more rows.

Ninth Tier of Blocks

Set up pat (RS): Sl 1, Seed pat over 23 sts, k18 C, Seed pat over 36 sts, k18 B, Seed pat over 36 sts, k18 A, Seed pat to end of row.

Keeping MC in Seed pat and colour blocks in St st, work even for 25 more rows.

10th Tier of Blocks

Set up pat (RS): Sl 1, Seed pat over 5 sts, k18 C, Seed pat over 36 sts, k18 B, Seed pat over 36 sts, k18 A, Seed pat to end of row.

Keeping MC in Seed pat and colour blocks in St st, work even for 25 more rows.

Top Border

With MC, work in Seed pat for 8 rows.

Bind off all sts.

Referring to charts, duplicate st letters on each colour block. ■

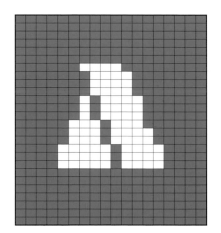
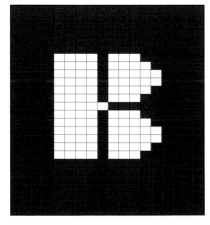
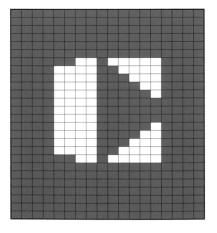

COLOUR KEY
☐ Natural
▨ Aqua
■ Fuchsia
▨ Lime

Spring Sky Layette

The gradual striping effect of this charming baby set will remind you of cottony clouds and soft blue skies.

Design | Laura Pulley

Skill Levels

Afghan and Hat: ■☐☐☐
BEGINNER

Sweater and Socks: ■■■☐
INTERMEDIATE

Sizes

Sweater: Infant 6 (12, 18, 24) months
Hat: Infant 0–6 (6–12, 12–24) months
Socks: Infant 6–12 (12–18, 18–24) months
Instructions are given for smallest size, with larger sizes in parentheses. When only 1 number is given, it applies to all sizes.

Finished Measurements

Sweater
Chest (buttoned): 23 (25, 27, 29) inches
Length: 11½ (14, 15, 16¾) inches

Hat
Circumference: 16¾ (18½, 20) inches

Socks
Foot length: 3¾ (4¼, 4¾) inches

Afghan
Approximately 31 x 41 inches

Materials

Worsted weight acrylic/wool blend yarn (200 yds/ 100g per ball):

Baby blue (MC):
    Sweater: 2 (2, 2, 3) balls
    Afghan: 3 balls
    Socks and hat: 1 ball will do both
Blue/yellow variegated (CC):
    Sweater: 2 (2, 2, 3) balls
    Afghan: 3 balls
    Socks and hat: 1 ball will do both
Size 6 (4mm) straight and double-pointed needles
Size 8 (5mm) straight and 29-inch circular needles or size needed to obtain gauge
Tapestry needle
⁹⁄₁₆-inch buttons: 6 (7, 8, 8)

Gauge

19 sts and 26 rows = 4 inches/10cm in St st and Stripe pat with larger needles
24 sts and 30 rnds = 4 inches/10cm in St st with dpns
To save time, take time to check gauge.

Special Abbreviation

M1 (Make 1): Insert LH needle from front to back under horizontal bar between st just worked and next st, lift this bar onto LH needle, then knit into back of it.

Pattern Stitches
A. Stripe Sequence (when worked in rows)

Row 1 (RS): With CC, knit.

Row 2: With CC, purl.

Row 3: With MC, knit.

Row 4: With MC, purl.

Rep Rows 1–4 for pat.

B. Stripe Sequence (when worked in rnds)

Rnds 1 and 2: With CC, knit.

Rnds 3 and 4: With MC, knit.

Rep Rnds 1–4 for pat.

Pattern Notes
Body of sweater is worked in 1 piece to armhole. Sleeves are worked flat, then joined to body for raglan yoke.

Circular needle is used to accommodate large number of sts; do not join but turn and work in rows throughout body of sweater. Work afghan in same manner.

Sweater instructions give buttonhole band for boys. If working sweater for girls, place buttonholes on right band.

First and last stitches of hat are used as selvage stitches.

Sweater

Sleeves
With smaller needles and MC, cast on 32 (32, 34, 36) sts.

Work in garter st for 9 rows, inc 2 (4, 4, 4) sts evenly spaced on last WS row. (34, 36, 38, 40 sts)

Change to larger needles and work Row 1 of Stripe pat across all sts.

Continue to work in Stripe pat, inc one st at each edge [every 6th row] 5 (6, 6, 7) times. (44, 48, 50, 54 sts)

Work even until sleeve measures 6 (7, 7½, 8½) inches, ending with a WS row.

Place first and last 5 sts on holder for armholes. Place remaining sts on 2nd holder.

Body
With smaller circular needle and MC, cast on 96 (104, 116, 120) sts.

Work in garter st for 9 rows, inc 12 (12, 12, 16) sts evenly spaced on last WS row. (108, 116, 128, 136 sts)

Change to larger needles, and work in Stripe pat until body measures approximately 5 (7, 7, 7½) inches, ending with a WS row and same colour stripe as last sleeve row.

Yoke
Next row (RS): Maintaining Stripe pat, k22 (24, 27, 29) sts for right front, pm, place next 10 sts on holder for right underarm, k34 (38, 40, 44) sts of first sleeve, pm, k44 (48, 54, 58) sts for back, pm, place next 10 sts on holder for left underarm, k34 (38, 40, 44) sts of 2nd sleeve, pm, k22 (24, 27, 29) sts for left front. (156, 172, 188, 204 sts)

Work even in established Stripe pat for 5 more rows.

Spring Sky Layette
Sample projects were knit with Encore (75 per cent acrylic/25 per cent wool) and Encore Colorspun (75 per cent acrylic/25 per cent wool) from Plymouth Yarn Co.

Begin raglan shaping

Dec row (RS): [Work to 3 sts before marker, ssk, k1, sl marker, k1, k2tog] 4 times, work to end of row. (8 st dec)

Continue in established pat, [working dec row every 4th row] 4 (4, 3, 4) times, then [every other row] 7 (8, 11, 12) times.

At the same time, when body measures 9½ (11, 12, 13¾) inches from lower edge, begin neck shaping.

Neck shaping

Bind off 8 (8, 8, 7) sts at beg of next 2 rows.

[Dec 1 st at each neck edge every other row] 2 (3, 4, 5) times. (40, 46, 44, 44 sts remain—(10, 12, 10, 10) for each sleeve and (20, 22, 24, 24) for back neck)

Note: On the last few dec rows, there will be insufficient sts at each edge to maintain the k1 st in between markers. Work these last dec as close to their original position as possible.

Work 1 row even. Place all sts on holder.

Neck Band

With RS facing using smaller needles and MC, beg at right front neck edge, pick up and knit 12 (13, 15, 16) sts along right front neck edge, k10 (12, 10, 10) sts of first sleeve, k20 (22, 24, 24) sts from back neck holder dec 2 sts evenly across back neck, k10 (12, 10, 10) sts of 2nd sleeve, pick up and knit 12 (13, 15, 16) sts along left front neck edge. (62, 70, 72, 74 sts)

Work in garter st for 9 rows.

Bind off purlwise on RS.

Button Band

With RS facing using smaller needles and MC, beg at lower edge of right front, pick up and knit 50 (56, 64, 70) sts evenly along front of sweater to top of neck band.

Knit 9 rows.

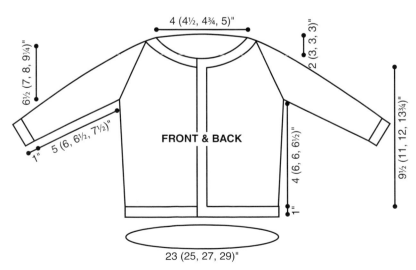

FRONT & BACK

6½ (7, 8, 9¼)"

4 (4½, 4¾, 5)"

2 (3, 3, 3)"

9½ (11, 12, 13¾)"

5 (6, 6½, 7½)"

1"

4 (6, 6, 6½)"

1"

23 (25, 27, 29)"

Bind off purlwise on RS.

Buttonhole Band
With RS facing using smaller needles and MC, beg at upper edge of left front neck band, pick up and knit 50 (56, 64, 70) sts evenly along front of sweater to lower edge of body.

Knit 3 rows.

Buttonhole row (RS):
6 months size only: K3, (yo, k2tog), [k6, yo, k2tog] 5 times, k3.

12 months size only: K3, (yo, k2tog), [k6, yo, k2tog] 6 times, k3.

18 months size only: K3, (yo, k2tog), [k6, yo, k2tog] 7 times, k3.

24 months size only: K3, (yo, k2tog), [k7, yo, k2tog] 7 times, k3.

Knit 5 more rows.

Bind off purlwise on RS.

Finishing
Join underarm sts of sleeves and body using Kitchener Stitch method, page 25.

Sew sleeve seams.

With CC and tapestry needle, work half-cross-st embroidery around all garter-st edges of sweater as shown in photo.

Work full cross-sts at corners of neck band and at sleeve seam.

Sew on buttons.

Hat

Body
With smaller needles and MC, cast on 73 (80, 86) sts.

Work in garter st for 9 rows, inc 9 (10, 12) sts evenly on last WS row. (82, 90, 98 sts)

Change to larger needles and work in Stripe pat until hat measures 4 (4½, 5) inches from beg, end with a WS row.

Shape crown
Row 1 (RS): K1 for selvage st, [k6, k2tog] 10 (11, 12) times, k1 for selvage st. (72, 79, 86 sts)

Row 2: Purl.

Row 3: K1 for selvage, [k5, k2tog] 10 (11, 12) times, k1 for selvage. (62, 68, 74 sts)

Row 4: Purl.

Continue in established pat, working decs every RS row as before, having 1 less st between each dec every time until 12 (13, 14) sts remaining, end with a WS row.

Finishing
Cut yarn. Draw end through remaining sts twice and draw tightly to close.

Sew back seam.

With CC and tapestry needle, work half cross-st embroidery around garter-st edge of hat as for sweater, working full cross-sts at hat seam.

Socks

Cuff
With MC and smaller straight needles, cast on 24 sts. Knit 11 rows, inc 4 sts evenly on last row. (28 sts)

With first dpn, [k1, p1] 4 times, k1.

With 2nd dpn, [p1, k1] 5 times.

With 3rd dpn, [p1, k1] 4 times, end p1.

Sts are now divided on 3 dpns as follows: 9 sts on first and 3rd needles and 10 sts on 2nd needle.

Pm and join.

Work 7 rnds more in k1, p1 rib as established.

Work 6 rnds in Stripe pat.

Cut CC.

Heel
With MC, k7 sts from first needle, turn, purl back across these 7 sts and purl 7 sts from 3rd needle. (14 sts on 1 needle)

Do not remove marker. Divide remaining 14 sts onto 2 needles for instep, to be worked later.

Working back and forth in rows on these 14 heel sts, work in St st for 13 rows, ending with a knit row.

Turn heel
Row 1 (WS): P8, p2tog, p1, turn.

Row 2: Sl 1, k3, ssk, k1, turn.

Row 3: Sl 1, p4, p2tog, p1, turn.

Row 4: Sl 1, k5, ssk, k1, turn.

Row 5: Sl 1, p6, p2tog, p1, turn.

Row 6: Sl 1, k6, ssk. Do not turn. (8 sts)

Shape gusset
With same needle used for Row 6 of heel turning, pick up and knit 9 sts along left edge of heel. With 2nd needle, knit across 14 instep sts. With 3rd needle, pick up and knit 9 sts along right edge of heel, then k4 sts from last needle. 40 sts are now divided on 3 needles as follows: 13 sts on first and 3rd needles, 14 sts on 2nd needle. Marker for beg of rnd is now at centre bottom of foot.

Knit 1 rnd.

Rnd 1: With CC, knit to last 3 sts of first needle, k2tog, k1, knit across 14 sts of 2nd needle, on 3rd needle k1, ssk, knit to end of rnd. (38 sts)

Rnd 2: Knit.

Maintaining Stripe pat, rep Rnds 1 and 2 until 28 sts remain.

Work even in established pat until foot measures approximately 2¾ (3¼, 3¾) inches from back of heel, ending with a full stripe.

Cut CC.

Toe
Rnd 1: With MC, knit to last 3 sts of first needle, k2tog, k1. On 2nd needle, k1, ssk, knit to last 3 sts, k2tog, k1. On 3rd needle, k1, ssk, knit to end of rnd.

Rnd 2: Knit.

Rep Rnds 1 and 2 until 12 sts remain, ending with Row 2.

Next row: K9, place 3 unworked sts of 3rd needle onto first needle.

Finishing
Cut MC, leaving an 8-inch end.

Graft tog 6 sts on either side of foot, using Kitchener Stitch, page 25.

Sew cuff seam. Turn cuff to RS.

With CC and tapestry needle, work half cross-st embroidery around garter-st cuff as for sweater, working full cross-sts at seam.

Afghan

Main Section
With smaller circular needle and MC, cast on 132 sts.

Knit 12 rows.

Inc row (WS): *K12, M1, rep from * across, end last rep k12. (142 sts)

Change to larger circular needle.

Work even in Stripe pat until main section measures approximately 39 inches from beg, end with a Row 2 of Stripe pat.

Cut CC and change to smaller circular needle.

Dec row (RS): With MC, [k11, k2tog] 10 times, k12. (132 sts)

Knit 13 rows.

Bind off purlwise on RS.

Side Borders
With smaller circular needle and MC, pick up and knit 184 sts along 1 side edge of main section, including garter-st sections.

Knit 13 rows.

Bind off purlwise on RS.

Rep for 2nd side.

Finishing
With tapestry needle and CC, working over middle 3 ridges of garter-st borders, work half cross-st embroidery around entire outer edge of afghan as for sweater, working full cross-sts at each corner. ∎

Embossed Ribs Baby Ensemble

Textured patterns and fish button accents highlight a slightly oversized baby sweater worked in colourful underwater hues.

Designs | Janet Rehfeldt

Skill Level

EASY

Sizes

Infant 6 (12, 18, 24) months

Instructions are given for smallest size, with larger sizes in parentheses. When only 1 number is given, it applies to all sizes.

Finished Measurements

Chest: 20 (22, 24, 26) inches
Total length: 9½ (11, 11¾, 13) inches
Hat circumference: 14 (15, 16, 17) inches
Booties heel to toe: 3½ (3¾, 4½, 5) inches
Foot circumference (unstretched): 4¾ (4¾, 5¼, 5¼) inches

Materials

Worsted weight mercerized cotton yarn (140 yds/100g per skein): 3 (3, 4, 4) skeins ocean

Size 7 (4.5mm) 16-inch circular and double-pointed needles

Size 8 (5mm) 16-inch circular and double-pointed needles or size needed to obtain gauge

Stitch holders

Stitch markers

Tapestry needle

4 (¾-inch) Streamline fish buttons from Blumenthal Lansing Co.

2 (size 4/0) snaps

Gauge

18 sts and 24 rows = 4 inches/10cm in Reverse St st on larger needles

To save time, take time to check gauge.

Pattern Stitch

Embossed Rib

Rnd 1: *K1-tbl; rep from * around.

Rnds 2–4: *P1, k1-tbl; rep from * around.

Rnd 5: *K1-tbl; rep from * around.

Rnds 6–8: K1-tbl, *p1, k1-tbl; rep from * around.

Rep Rnds 1–8 for pat.

Pattern Notes

Sweater is worked in the round to the underarm, then worked back and forth for the upper bodice.

Hat is worked in the round using circular and double-pointed needles.

Booties are worked in the round using double-pointed needles. For ease in working, use shorter 5–6-inch size.

Embossed Ribs Baby Ensemble
Sample projects were knit with Fantasy
Naturale (100 per cent cotton) from
Plymouth Yarn Co.

Pullover

Body

With smaller needles, cast on 96 (102, 108, 114) sts.

Join without twisting, pm between first and last st.

Work in k1, p1 rib for 4 rnds.

Next rnd: Knit, inc 12 (14, 16, 18) sts evenly. (108, 116, 124, 132 sts)

Change to larger needles and Embossed Rib pat.

[Work rnds 1–8] 2 (3, 3, 4) times, then [work rnds 1–4] 1 (0, 1, 0) times.

Divide for front and back

Purl 1 rnd, dec 4 sts evenly. (104, 112, 120, 128 sts)

Back

Next row (RS): Purl across 52 (56, 60, 64) sts, sl remaining sts to holder.

Work even in rows from this point in Reverse St st until armhole measures 4 (4½, 5, 5½) inches, ending with a RS row.

Shape neck

K18 (19, 20, 21) sts, sl 16 (18, 20, 22) back neck sts to holder, attach 2nd ball of yarn, knit remaining 18 (19, 20, 21) sts.

Next row: Dec 1 st at each neck edge.

Work 4 rows even for button extension.

Bind off 17 (18, 19, 20) sts on each shoulder.

Front

Sl 52 (56, 60, 64) sts from holder onto larger needles.

With RS facing, join yarn and purl across.

Work even in Reverse St st until armhole measures 2½ (3, 3, 3½) inches.

Shape neck

Work across 22 (23, 25, 26) sts, sl centre 8 (10, 10, 12) sts to holder for front neck, attach 2nd ball of yarn and work across remaining 22 (23, 25, 26) sts.

[Dec 1 st each side of neck every row] 5 (5, 6, 6) times. (17, 18, 19, 20 sts on each side)

Work even until armhole measures 4¼ (4½, 4¾, 5) inches, ending with a WS.

Beg buttonhole band

Mark each shoulder for 2 buttonholes, evenly spaced.

Work in k1, p1 rib for 5 rows, making buttonholes on Row 3 by working [yo, k2tog] at each marker.

Bind off all sts.

Back Neck Band

With smaller needles and RS facing, join yarn at right shoulder, pick up and knit 5 sts along button placket and right neck edge, 16 (18, 20, 22) sts from back neck holder and 5 sts along left button placket and neck edge. (26, 28, 30, 32 sts)

Work in k1, p1 rib for 4 rows.

Bind off.

Front Neck Band

With smaller needles and RS facing, join yarn at left shoulder, pick up and knit 10 (12, 14, 15) sts along buttonhole band and left neck edge, 8 (10, 10, 12) sts from front neck holder and 10 (12, 14, 15) sts along right buttonhole band and neck edge. (28, 32, 38, 42 sts)

Work in k1, p1 rib for 4 rows.

Bind off.

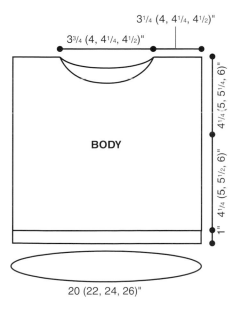

3¾ (4, 4¼, 4½)"
3¼ (4, 4¼, 4½)"

BODY

4¼ (5, 5¼, 6)"
4¼ (5, 5½, 6)"
1"

20 (22, 24, 26)"

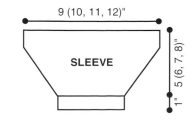

9 (10, 11, 12)"

SLEEVE

5 (6, 7, 8)"
1"

Sleeves

With smaller needles, cast on 26 (28, 30, 34) sts.

Work in k1, p1 rib for 4 rows.

Change to larger needles and Reverse St st.

[Inc 1 st each side every 3rd row] 8 (3, 3, 1) times, then [every 4th row] 0 (5, 7, 9) times. (42, 44, 50, 54 sts)

Work even until sleeve measures 6 (7, 8, 9) inches.

Bind off loosely.

Finishing

Lap buttonhole band over button extension. Sew sleeve top to armhole, easing to fit and sewing through all layers at shoulder.

Sew sleeve seams.

Sew buttons to button band.

Sew one snap to each side of neck band near bound-off edge.

Hat

Border

With smaller dpn, cast on 64 (68, 72, 76) sts.

Join without twisting, pm between first and last st.

Work in k1, p1 rib for 4 rnds.

Body

Change to larger needles and Embossed Rib pat.

Rnd 7: *P6, p2tog; rep from * around. (42, 42, 49, 49 sts)

Rnd 9: *P5, p2tog; rep from * around. (36, 36, 42, 42 sts)

Rnd 11: *P4, p2tog; rep from * around. (30, 30, 35, 35 sts)

Rnd 13: *P3, p2tog; rep from * around. (24, 24, 28, 28 sts)

Rnd 15: *P2, p2tog; rep from * around. (18, 18, 21, 21 sts)

Next rnd: *P1, p2tog; rep from * around. (12, 12, 14, 14 sts)

Cut yarn, leaving a 12-inch end.

Draw end through remaining sts twice and pull tightly.

Weave in end.

Booties

Cuff & Leg
With smaller dpn, cast on 22 (22, 24, 24) sts.

Divide sts onto 3 needles as follows: 5-12-5, (5-12-5, 6-12-6, 6-12-6)

Join without twisting, pm between first and last st.

Work in k1, p1 rib for 3 rnds. Knit 1 rnd.

Work Rnds 1–8.

Heel Flap
Place instep sts of 2nd needle on holder for ease in working heel.

Work Rnds 1–8, then work [Rnds 1–4] 0 (0, 1, 1) time.

Purl 1 rnd, dec 2 sts evenly. (62, 66, 70, 74 sts)

Work even in Reverse St st until hat measures 3 (3½, 4, 4½) inches from beg.

Shape crown
Change to dpn when necessary.

Rnd 1: [P29 (9, 0, 17), p2tog] 2 (6, 0, 4) times. (60, 60, 70, 70 sts)

Rnd 2 and all even-numbered rnds: Purl.

Rnd 3: *P8, p2tog; rep from * around. (54, 54, 63, 63 sts)

Rnd 5: *P7, p2tog; rep from * around. (48, 48, 56, 56 sts)

Knit sts of 1st needle onto 3rd needle. Turn.

Work back and forth across 10 (10, 12, 12) heel sts, turning work after each row as follows:

Row 1: Sl 1, purl across.

Row 2: Sl 1, knit across.

Rep Rows 1–2 until heel flap measures approximately 1 (1¼, 1½, 1½) inches, ending with a WS row.

Turn heel
Row 1: K5 (5, 7, 7), ssk, k1, turn.

Row 2: Sl 1, p2 (2, 4, 4), p2tog, p1, turn.

Row 3: Sl 1, k3 (3, 4, 4), ssk, k1, turn.

Row 4: Sl 1, p3 (3, 5, 5), p2tog, p1, turn.

Row 5: Sl 1, k3 (3, 5, 5), ssk, turn.

Row 6: Sl 1, p2 (2, 4, 4), p2tog. (4, 4, 6, 6 sts)

Shape gusset
Sl instep sts from holder to 2nd needle.

K4 (4, 6, 6) heel sts, with same needle pick up and knit 7 (8, 10, 10) sts along left side of heel flap, with 2nd needle purl across instep sts, with 3rd needle pick up and knit 7 (8, 10, 10) sts along right side of heel flap, knit half of heel sts onto last needle.

You should have 9 (10, 13, 13) sts on 1st needle and 3rd needle, and 12 sts on 2nd needle.

Rnd 1: On 1st needle, purl to last 3 sts, then p2tog, p1; on 2nd needle, purl all sts; on 3rd needle, p1, p2tog, purl to end of rnd.

Rnd 2: Purl.

Rep Rnds 1–2 until 22 (22, 24, 24) sts remain.

Foot
Work even in Reverse St st until foot measures 3 (3¼, 4, 4½) inches from back of heel or ½ inch less than desired length.

Shape toe
Rearrange sts so there are 5-11-6 (5-11-6, 6-12-6, 6-12-6) sts on needles.

Dec rnd: On first needle, purl to last 3 sts, p2tog, p1; on second needle, p1, p2tog, purl to last 3 sts, p2tog, p1; on third needle, p1, p2tog, purl to end of rnd.

Rep dec rnd 3 times. (10, 10, 12, 12 sts)

Sizes 18 and 24 months only: On 1st needle, purl to last 3 sts, p2tog, p1; on 2nd needle, purl to last 3 sts, p2tog, p1; on 3rd needle, purl all sts without dec. (10 sts)

Cut yarn.

Weave toe sts tog using Kitchener Stitch method, page 25. ■

GARTER STRIPES ENSEMBLE

Playful eye-catching stripes ensure that Baby will enjoy attention. Leg warmers add a fashionable, yet practical touch.

Designs | Scarlet Taylor

Skill Level
EASY

Sizes
Cardigan: Infant 6 (12, 18) months
Hat: Infant 6 (12–18) months
Leg Warmers: Infant 6–12 (18) months
For each project, instructions are given for smallest size with larger size(s) in parentheses. When only 1 number is given, it applies to both (all) sizes.

Finished Measurements
Cardigan
Chest: 22 (24, 26) inches
Length: 9½ (11, 12) inches
Blanket
30 x 33 inches
Hat
Circumference: 15½ (16½) inches
Depth: 5½ (6) inches
Leg warmer
Circumference at ankle: 6½ (7) inches
Circumference at knee: 8½ (9) inches
Length: 7½ (8½) inches

Materials
Worsted weight yarn (200 yds/100g per ball):
   For cardigan: 1 ball each white #146 (A), lilac #1308 (B), light green #450 (C), pink #449 (D) and peach #448 (E)

4 MEDIUM

For blanket: 2 balls white #146 (A), 1 ball each lilac #1308 (B), light green #450 (C), pink #449 (D) and peach #448 (E)
For hat and legwarmers: 1 ball each white #146 (A), lilac #1308 (B), light green #450 (C), pink #449 (D) and peach #448 (E)
Size 6 (4.25mm) straight needles
Size 8 (5mm) straight and 29-inch circular needles or size needed to obtain gauge
Stitch holders
Stitch markers
Tapestry needle
4 (6, 6) ¾-inch buttons

Gauge
16 sts and 32 rows = 4 inches/10cm in pat st with larger needles
To save time, take time to check gauge.

Pattern Stitch
Garter Stripes
Rows 1 (RS)–4: With B, knit. Cut B.

Row 5: With A, knit.

Row 6: With A, purl. Do not cut.

Rows 7–10: With C, knit. Cut C.

Garter Stripes Ensemble
Sample projects were knit with Encore
Worsted (75 per cent acrylic/25 per cent
wool) from Plymouth Yarn Co.

Rows 11 and 12: Rep Rows 5 and 6.

Rows 13–16: With D, knit. Cut D.

Rows 17 and 18: Rep Rows 5 and 6.

Rows 19–22: With E, knit. Cut E.

Rows 23 and 24: Rep Rows 5 and 6.

Rep Rows 1–24 for pat.

Pattern Notes

Cardigan body is worked in 1 piece to the armholes, then divided to complete fronts and back separately.

Carry A loosely up side; cut other colours and weave in loose ends.

Cardigan

Body
Bottom edge

With smaller straight needles and B, cast on 88 (96, 104) sts.

Work in garter st for approx ½ inch, ending with a WS row.

Next row (RS): Change to larger straight needles, and beg with row 1, work even in Garter Stripes until piece measures 5 (6¼, 6¾) inches from beg, ending with a WS row.

Divide for fronts & back

Next row (RS): Work 22 (24, 26) sts and place on holder for right front; work next 44 (48, 52) sts for back; place rem 22 (24, 26) sts on holder for left front.

Back

Next row (WS): Working on back sts only, continue in pat as established, and work 1 row.

Shape armholes

Bind off 3 (4, 5) sts at beg of next 2 rows. (38, 40, 42 sts)

Work even until piece measures 9¼ (10¾, 11¾) inches from beg, ending with a WS row.

Shape back neck

Work 12 (13, 13) sts, join a 2nd ball of yarn and bind off centre 14 (14, 16) sts for back neck, work to end.

Working both sides at once with separate balls of yarn, dec 1 st at each neck edge once. Bind off rem 11 (12, 12) sts each side for shoulders.

Right Front

Sl sts for right front to needle with WS facing and attach yarn.

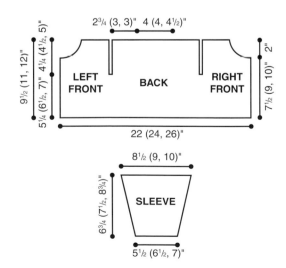

Shape armhole
Next row (WS): Bind off 3 (4, 5) sts, work in pat to end of row. (19, 20, 21 sts)

Work even until piece measures 7½ (9, 10) inches from beg, ending with a WS row.

Shape front neck
Next row (RS): Bind off 3 sts, work in pat to end of row. (16, 17, 18 sts)

18-Month Size Only
Bind off 2 sts at beg of next RS row.

All sizes
Dec 1 st at neck edge every RS row 5 (5, 4) times. (11, 12, 12 sts)

Work even until piece measures same as back to shoulders.

Bind off.

Left Front
Sl sts for left front to needle with RS facing and attach yarn.

Shape armhole
Next row (RS): Bind off 3 (4, 5) sts, work in pat to end of row. (19, 20, 21 sts)

Work even until piece measures 7½ (9, 10) inches from beg, ending with a RS row.

Shape front neck
Next row (WS): Bind off 3 sts, work in pat to end of row. (16, 17, 18 sts)

18-Month Size Only
Bind off 2 sts at beg of next WS row.

All sizes
Dec 1 st at neck edge every RS row 5 (5, 4) times. (11, 12, 12 sts)

Work even until piece measures same as back to shoulders.

Bind off.

Sleeves
With smaller needles and B, cast on 22 (26, 28) sts.

Work in garter st for approx ½ inch, ending with a WS row.

Next row (RS): Change to larger needles, and beg with Row 1, work Garter Stripes pat; *at the same time*, inc 1 st each side on this row, then [every 6th row] 5 (1, 1) time(s), then [every 8 row] 0 (3, 4) times. (34, 36, 40 sts)

Work even until piece measures 6¾ (7½, 8¾) inches from beg, ending with a WS row.

Bind off.

Assembly
Sew shoulder seams.

Neckband

With RS facing, using smaller needles and B, pick up and knit 49 (49, 51) sts evenly around neck edge.

Work in garter st for approx 1 inch.

Bind off loosely.

Button band

Note: Work on left front edge for girl/right front edge for boy.

With RS facing, using smaller needles and B, pick up and knit 41 (48, 53) sts evenly along edge including neckband.

Work in garter st for approx 1 inch.

Bind off loosely.

Place markers for 4 (6, 6) buttons evenly spaced, with first and last buttons ½ inch from top and bottom edges of cardigan.

Buttonhole band

Note: Work on right front edge for girl/left front edge for boy.

Work as for button band until band measures approx ½ inch.

Next row: Make buttonholes opposite markers by working yo, k2tog.

Work even until band measures approx 1 inch.

Bind off loosely.

Finishing

Sew in sleeves; sew sleeve seams.

Sew on buttons. Wash and block.

Blanket

Pattern Note

A circular needle is used to accommodate large number of sts. Do not join; work the blanket back and forth in rows.

Border

With A, cast on 120 sts.

Work in garter st for approx 1 inch, ending with a WS row.

Set up side borders: With A, k4, place marker, join B and work Garter Stripes to last 4 sts, place marker, join a 2nd ball of A, k4.

Continue in pats as established, maintaining first and last 4 sts in garter st in A for side borders throughout, until blanket measures approx 34 inches from beg, ending with Row 4 of Garter Stripes pat.

Next row (RS): With A only, work in garter st for approx 1 inch, ending with a WS row. Bind off loosely knitwise.

Finishing

Weave in yarn ends.

Hat

Rolled edge

With B, cast on 80 (84) sts.

Work in St st for approx 1¼ inches, ending with a WS row.

Body
Beg st pat & dec for hat
Next row: Beg Garter Stripes and dec across as follows: k2 (4), k2tog, [k3, k2tog] 15 times, k1 (3). (64, 68 sts)

Work even for approx 4¼ (4¾) inches, ending with a WS row.

Cut yarns and continue in B only.

Shape crown
Dec row 1 (RS): K6, k2tog, [k3, k2tog] 10 (11) times, k6 (5). (53, 56 sts)

Next row and all WS rows: Knit.

Dec row 2: K6 (5), k2tog, [k2, k2tog] 10 (11) times, k5. (42, 44 sts)

Dec row 3: K5, k2tog, [k1, k2tog] 10 (11) times, k5 (4). (31, 32 sts)

Dec row 4: K1 (2), k2tog, [k1, k2tog] 9 times, k1. (21, 22 sts)

Dec row 5: K1, [k2tog] 9 (10) times, k2 (1). (12 sts)

I-Cord tails
Knit 4 I-cord tails using a different colour for each tail as follows:

Sl last 9 sts to holder.

Join desired colour and *k3; do not turn, sl sts back to LH needle; rep from * until cord is 2½ inches or desired length.

Bind off.

Using different colours, make 3 more 3-st I-cord tails using rem 9 sts.

Finishing
With WS facing, sew seam of rolled edge.

With RS facing, sew rest of seam to top, matching pat.

Weave in yarn ends.

Leg warmers

With smaller straight needles and B, cast on 26 (28) sts.

Work in k1, p1 rib until piece measures approx ½ inch, ending with a WS row.

Change to larger straight needles and Garter Stripes.

Shape leg
Inc 1 st each side [every 10th row] 2 (0) times, then [every 12th row] 2 (2) times, then [every 14th row] 0 (2) times. (34, 36 sts)

Work even until piece measures approx 7 (8) inches from beg, ending with a WS row.

Change to smaller needles and B, then work in k1, p1 rib for approx ½ inch.

Bind off loosely in rib.

Finishing
Sew leg seam matching pat.

Weave in loose ends. ∎

ON-THE-GO BABY SET

This contemporary colour-block design is equally wonderful in bright colours to stimulate baby or in soft colours to soothe.

Designs | Kathy Perry

Skill Level
EASY

Sizes

Infant 6 (12, 18) months Instructions are given for smallest size, with larger sizes in parentheses. When only 1 number is given, it applies to all sizes.

Finished Measurements
Sweater
Chest: 20 (21, 22) inches
Length: 11½ (12½, 13½) inches
Hat
Circumference: 16 (17, 17) inches
Blanket
30 x 35 inches

Materials

Worsted weight yarn (315 yds/6 oz per skein):
   For sweater and hat: 1 skein each limelight #9607 (A), berry blue #9609 (B) and lemonade #9606 (C)
   For blanket: 1 skein each limelight #9607 (A), berry blue #9609 (B) and lemonade #9606 (C)
Size 8 (5mm) straight needles and 29-inch circular needle (blanket only) or size needed to obtain gauge
Size 10 (6mm) 16-inch circular needle (sweater collar only)
Size H/8 (5mm) crochet hook (for blanket only)

Stitch holders
Tapestry needle
Needle and thread

Gauge

18 sts and 24 rows = 4 inches/10cm in St st
To save time, take time to check gauge.

Sweater

Back/Front
Make 2 alike
With straight needles and A, cast on 48 (50, 52) sts.

Work even in K1, P1 Rib (see page 19) until piece measures 7½ (8¼, 9) inches, ending with a WS row.

Change to B and work even for 2 (2¼, 2½) inches, ending with a WS row.

Shape neck & shoulders
Work 19 (20, 21) sts; sl the next 10 sts to a holder; with a 2nd ball of yarn, work rem 19 (20, 21) sts.

Working both sides at once, dec 1 at neck edge [every row] 5 times. (14, 15, 16 sts)

On-the-Go Baby Set
Sample projects were knit with
Simply Soft Brites (100 per cent
acrylic) from Caron International.

Work even until armhole (section in B) measures 4 (4¼, 4½) inches.

Bind off.

Sleeves
With straight needles and C, cast on 25 (27, 29) sts.

Work K1, P1 Rib for 1½ inches.

Change to A and St st.

Inc 1 st each side [every 5 rows] 6 (5, 6) times, then [every 0 (6, 0) rows] 0 (1, 0) time(s). (37, 39, 41 sts)

Work even until sleeve measures 6½ (7½, 8) inches from beg.

Bind off all sts.

Assembly
Sew shoulder seams.

Collar
With RS facing, using larger circular needle and C, and beg in centre of sts on front neck holder, k5 across (right) front neck holder, pick up and knit 10 sts from right-front neck edge and 10 sts from right-back neck edge, k10 from back neck holder, pick up and knit 10 sts from left-back neck edge and 10 sts from left-front neck edge, knit 4 sts from (left) front neck holder, then knit in front and back of last st on holder. (61 sts)

Work in K1, P1 Rib for 3½ inches.

Bind off all sts very loosely.

Sew sleeves to upper section in B. Sew side and underarm seams. Let bottom edge roll naturally.

Finishing

Weave in all ends and block to measurements.

Hat

Hem

With straight needles and A, cast on 73 (78, 78) sts.

Work in St st for 4 inches.

Body

Change to B and work in St st for 3 inches, ending with a WS row.

Next row: *K3, k2tog; rep from * across, end k3. (59, 63, 63 sts)

Work even until B measures 6 (6½, 7) inches.

Bind off, leaving a 15-inch tail.

Finishing

Using tail end, make a running st through top row of sts, gathering tightly.

Using same tail, sew back seam of B section, then use A to sew back seam of A section.

Fold bottom half of hem to WS and tack in place at colour-change row.

Make 1 medium-sized (about 2½ inch diameter) pompom in each colour; join the 3 pompoms tog to make 1 large pompom and sew to top.

Using 3 strands of A, braid a cord 8 inches long. Make 2 small pompoms (about 1 inch diameter), 1 each in A and C and attach to ends of braid. Tie braid around large pompom.

Blanket

Pattern Notes

The blanket is worked back and forth; a circular needle is used to accommodate the large number of sts.

This blanket is worked using separate balls of yarn for each coloured section; bring new colour up from under old colour to lock them.

Border

With smaller circular needle and C, cast on 148 sts.

Work even in St st for 2½ inches, ending with a WS row. Cut C.

Squares

Change to A and k74, drop A; join B and k74 sts.

Work even in St st with 74 sts in A and 74 sts in B until A/B section measures 15 inches, ending with a WS row.

Next row (RS): K74 B, k74 A.

Work even until B/A section measures 15 inches, ending with a WS row. Cut A and B.

Border

Change to C and work even for 2½ inches.

Bind off.

Finishing
Side Hems

Turn over 6 sts along the side edges and tack down using needle and thread.

With C, work 2 rows single crochet along top and bottom edges.

With C, make 10 pompoms and sew 5 each to top and bottom borders, about 1½ inch from edge. ■

Pompoms

Cut two cardboard circles in size specified in pattern. Cut a hole in the centre of each circle, about ½ inch in diameter. Thread a tapestry needle with a length of yarn doubled. Holding both circles together, insert needle through centre hole, over the outside edge, through centre again (Fig. 1) until entire circle is covered and centre hole is filled (thread more length of yarn as needed).

Fig. 1

With sharp scissors, cut yarn between the two circles all around the circumference (Fig. 2).

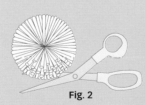

Fig. 2

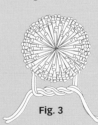

Fig. 3

Using two 12-inch strands of yarn, slip yarn between circles and overlap yarn ends two or three times (Fig. 3) to prevent knot from slipping, pull tightly and tie into a firm knot. Remove cardboard and fluff out pompom by rolling it between your hands. Trim even with scissors, leaving tying ends for attaching pompom to project.

SPUN SUGAR BABY SET

A delicate hem and lovely lace are easy to create with simple yarn overs.

Designs | Frances Hughes

Skill Level

EASY

Size
Newborn

Finished Measurement
Chest: 18 inches

Materials
DK weight nylon/acrylic blend yarn (193 yds/50g per ball): 2 balls pink
Size 4 (3.5mm) needles
Size 5 (3.75mm) needles or size needed to obtain gauge
Stitch markers
Stitch holders
2 yds ⅛-inch pink satin ribbon (for bonnet)
3 (¼-inch) buttons (for sweater)

Gauge
24 sts and 30 rows = 4 inches/10cm in St st with larger needles
To save time, take time to check gauge.

Pattern Stitch
Eyelet Lace (multiple of 6 sts + 1)

Row 1 (RS): K1, *yo, p1, p3tog, p1, yo, k1; rep from * across.

Row 2 and all WS rows: Purl.

Row 3: K2, yo, sl 1, k2tog, psso, yo, *k3, yo, sl 1, k2tog, psso, yo; rep from * to last 2 sts, end k2.

Row 5: P2tog, p1, yo, k1, yo, p1, *p3tog, p1, yo, k1, yo, p1; rep from * to last 2 sts, end p2tog.

Row 7: K2tog, yo, k3, yo, *sl 1, k2tog, psso, yo, k3, yo; rep from * to last 2 sts, end ssk.

Rows 9 and 10: Rep Rows 1 and 2.

Pattern Note
Yarn amount given will make entire set.

Bonnet

Hem
With larger needles, cast on 63 sts.

Row 1: Knit.

Row 2: K4, purl to last 4 sts, k4.

Rows 3 and 4: Rep Rows 1 and 2.

Row 5: K1, *yo, k2tog; rep from * across. (Fold row for hem)

Rows 6 and 8: K4, purl to last 4 sts, k4.

Rows 7 and 9: Knit.

Row 10: Rep Row 6. (Hem completed)

Body
Beg lace pat (RS): K4, place marker, k1, [yo, p1, p3tog, p1, yo, k1] 9 times (Row 1 of Eyelet Lace pat), place marker, k4.

Row 2 and all WS rows: K4, purl to last 4 sts, k4.

Rows 3–10: Continue to work in established pat between markers, keeping 4 sts at each edge in garter st.

Row 11: Knit.

Row 12: K4, purl to last 4 sts, k4.

Rep Rows 11 and 12 until piece measures 4¼ inches from cast-on edge.

Shape crown
Row 1: *K7, k2tog; rep from * across. (56 sts)

Row 2 and all WS rows: Purl.

Row 3: *K6, k2tog; rep from * across. (49 sts)

Row 5: *K5, k2tog; rep from * across. (42 sts)

Continue to dec in this manner, having 1 st less between dec until 7 sts rem.

Cut yarn, leaving a 10-inch tail. Run end through rem sts, pull tight, then sew back edges tog from centre to beg of crown shaping. Fasten off.

Ties
Cut 2 (12-inch) pieces of ribbon, sew to front corners of bonnet.

Sweater

Note: Sweater is worked in 1 piece to underarm.

Body
Hem
With larger needles, cast on 105 sts.

Referring to bonnet instructions, work Rows 1–10 of Hem.

Beg lace pat (RS): K4, place marker, k1, [yo, p1, p3tog, p1, yo, k1] 16 times (Row 1 of Eyelet Lace pat), place marker, k4.

Work Rows 2–12 for Eyelet Lace pat as for bonnet, then work in St st, keeping 4 sts at each edge in garter st until body measures 6¼ inches from beg, ending with a WS row.

Divide for yoke
Row 1: With RS facing, k2, yo, k2tog (buttonhole), k23, turn, leaving rem sts unworked. (27 sts)

Rows 2, 4 and 6: P23, k4.

Rows 3 and 5: Knit.

Row 7: K2, yo, k2tog (buttonhole), k23.

Rows 8–12: Rep Rows 2–6.

Row 13: K2, yo, k2tog (buttonhole), sl these 4 sts onto a holder, k2tog, k21.

Spun Sugar Baby Set
Sample projects were knit with Sirdar Snuggly DK (55 per cent acrylic/45 per cent wool) from Knitting Fever Inc.

Row 14: P20, p2tog-tbl, turn.

Rows 15–20: Work in St st, dec 1 st at neck edge every row. (15 sts)

Rows 21–24: Work even in St st.

Place these 15 sts on a holder.

Back
With RS facing, attach yarn at underarm. Work in St st on next 51 sts for 24 rows. Place sts on holder, marking centre 21 sts for back neck.

Left Front
Row 1: With RS facing, attach yarn at underarm, k27.

Row 2: K4, p23.

Rows 3–12: Rep Rows 1 and 2.

Row 13: K21, k2tog, place last 4 sts on holder, turn.

Row 14: P2tog, p20, turn.

Rows 15–20: Work in St st, dec 1 st at neck edge every row. (15 sts)

Rows 21–24: Work even in St st.

Place these 15 sts on a holder.

Sleeves
Hem
With larger needles, cast on 31 sts.

Row 1 (RS): Knit.

Row 2: Purl.

Rows 3 and 4: Rep Rows 1 and 2.

Row 5: K1, *yo, k2tog; rep from * across. (Fold row for hem)

Rows 6 and 8: Purl.

Rows 7 and 9: Knit.

Row 10: Rep Row 6. (Hem completed)

Beg lace pat (RS): K1, [yo, p1, p3tog, p1, yo, k1] 5 times (Row 1 of Eyelet Lace pat).

Work Rows 2–10 of Eyelet Lace pat.

Beg with a knit row, work in St st until sleeve measures 5¾ inches from cast-on edge. Bind off all sts.

Sew underarm seam. Fold and sew hem in place.

Assembly
Fold lower hem and sew in place.

Join front and back shoulder sts using 3-Needle Bind-Off, page 26.

Set sleeves into armholes.

Neck band
With RS facing, sl 4 sts from holder onto needle, attach yarn, k4, pick up and knit 12 sts along right front neck,

knit across back neck sts, pick up and knit 12 sts along left front neck edge, knit 4 sts from holder. (53 sts)

Knit 4 rows. Bind off all sts.

Attach buttons opposite buttonholes, block lightly.

Booties

Cuff
Note: Inc by knitting in front and back of st.

With smaller needles, cast on 37 sts.

Row 1: K1, inc in next st, k15, inc in next st, k1, inc in next st, k15, inc in next st, k1. (41 sts)

Row 2: Knit.

Row 3: K1, inc in next st, k17, inc in next st, k1, inc in next st, k17, inc in next st, k1. (45 sts)

Row 4: Knit.

Row 5: K1, inc in next st, k19, inc in next st, k1, inc in next st, k19, inc in next st, k1. (49 sts)

Rows 6–15: Knit.

Foot
Shape instep
Row 1: K10, p18, p3tog, turn.

Row 2: Sl 1, k7, sl 1, k2tog, psso, turn.

Row 3: Sl 1, p7, p3tog, turn.

Rows 4–10: Rep Rows 2 and 3, ending with a Row 2. Do not turn, but knit rem 10 sts on left needle. (29 sts)

Next row: Knit across, inc 2 sts evenly. (31 sts)

Eyelet row: K1, *yo, k2tog; rep from * across.

Next row: Knit.

Beg lace pat (RS): K1, [yo, p1, p3tog, p1, yo, k1] 5 times (Row 1 of Eyelet Lace pat).

Work Rows 2–10 of Eyelet Lace pat.

Beg with a knit row, work 3 rows St st, rep eyelet row, then work 4 rows St st.

Bind off all sts.

Sew seam from bottom of foot to top of cuff. Fold hem to inside, sew loosely in place. Cut 2 (18-inch) pieces of ribbon, thread through eyelet row and tie ends in a bow. ■

PRECIOUS BABY JACKET & CUBE

Designed for the best-dressed, playful baby, this sweater is quick and easy to complete.

Design | E.J. Slayton

Skill Level
EASY

Jacket

Sizes

Infant 6 (12, 18) months. Instructions are given for smallest size, with larger sizes in parentheses. When only 1 number is given, it applies to all sizes.

Finished Measurements

Chest: 22 (25, 27½) inches
Length: 11 (11¾, 12½) inches

Materials

Worsted weight acrylic yarn (241 yds/100g per ball): 2 balls aqua
Size 6 (4mm) needles or size needed to obtain gauge
Stitch markers
Stitch holders
1 (⅝-inch) button

4 MEDIUM

Special Abbreviations

K1B (knit 1 in row below):
K1 in st 1 row below st on LH needle, sl both sts off LH needle. (Fig. 1)
M1 (make 1): Inc by making a backward lp over right needle.

Fig. 1

Pattern Stitch

Little Bows (multiple of 6 sts + 5)

Row 1 (WS): P1, k3, *p3, k3; rep from * to last st, end p1.

Row 2: K1, p1, k1B, p1, *k3, p1, k1B, p1; rep from * to last st, end k1.

Row 3: Purl.

Row 4: Knit.

Row 5: P4, k3, *p3, k3; rep from * to last 4 sts, end p4.

Row 6: K4, p1, k1B, p1, *k3, p1, k1B, p1; rep from * to last 4 sts, end k4.

Rows 7 and 8: Rep Rows 3 and 4.

Rep Rows 1–8 for pat.

Gauge

17 sts and 24 rows = 4 inches/10cm in pat
To save time, take time to check gauge.

Pattern Note

When increasing or decreasing, work any partial pattern repeats in Stockinette stitch.

**Precious Baby
Jacket & Cube**

Sample projects were knit
with Canadiana (100 per
cent acrylic) from Patons.

Back

Cast on 47 (53, 59) sts. Beg with a WS row, knit 6 rows (3 ridges of garter st), inc 1 st at each edge on last row. (49, 55, 61 sts)

Purl 1 row, knit 1 row.

Row 1 (WS): P2, k3, *p3, k3; rep from * to last 2 sts, end p2.

Row 2: K2, p1, k1B, p1, *k3, p1, k1B, p1; rep from * to last 2 sts, end k2.

Work in established pat until back measures approx 4 (4½, 5) from beg, ending with Row 3 or 7.

Shape sides

Beg on next row and maintaining established pat, dec 1 st at each side (k1, ssk, knit to last 3 sts, k2tog, k1) [every 8th row] 3 times. (43, 49, 55 sts)

Work even until back measures approx 7 (7½, 8) inches from beg, ending with a WS row.

Shape armhole

Bind off 4 sts at beg of next 2 rows, then work even on rem 35 (41, 47) sts until armhole measures approx 4 (4¼, 4¾) inches from underarm, ending with Row 3 or 7. Mark centre 17 (17, 19) sts for back neck, place sts on holder or spare needle.

Right Front

Cast on 23 (29, 35) sts and work garter st edge as for back, inc 1 st at each edge. (25, 31, 37 sts)

Purl 1 row, knit 1 row.

Row 1 (WS): P2, k3, *p3, k3; rep from * to last 2 sts, end p2.

Row 2: K2, p1, k1B, p1, *k3, p1, k1B, p1; rep from * to last 2 sts, end k2.

Work in established pat until front measures approx 4 (4½, 5) from beg, ending with Row 3 or 7.

Shape side

Beg on next row and maintaining established pat, dec 1 st at end of row (knit to last 3 sts, k2tog, k1) [every 8th row] 3 times. (22, 28, 34 sts)

Work even until front measures approx 7 (7½, 8) inches from beg, ending with a RS row.

Shape armhole

Bind off 4 sts at beg of next row, then work even on rem 18 (24, 30) sts until armhole measures approx 2 (2¼, 2½) inches from underarm, ending with a WS row.

Shape neck

Knit first 3 (6, 10) sts and place on holder, knit to end of row. Maintaining established pat, dec 1 st at neck edge (k1, ssk, knit across) [every RS row] 3 times, then work even on rem 12 (15, 17) sts until front measures same as back to shoulder. Place shoulder sts on holder.

Left Front

Cast on 23 (29, 35) sts and work as for right front to beg of side shaping.

Shape side

Beg on next row and maintaining established pat, dec 1 st at beg of row (k1, ssk, knit across) [every 8th row] 3 times. (22, 28, 34 sts)

Work even until front measures approx 7 (7½, 8) inches from beg, ending with a WS row.

Shape armhole

Bind off 4 sts at beg of next row, then work even on rem 18 (24, 30) sts until armhole measures approx 2 (2¼, 2½) inches from underarm, ending 3 (6, 10) sts from end of RS row. Place these sts on a holder.

Shape neck

Continue to work in pat, dec 1 st at neck edge (knit to last 3 sts, k2tog, k1) [every RS row] 3 times, then work even on rem 12 (15, 17) sts until front measures same as back to shoulder. Place shoulder sts on holder.

Sleeves

Cast on 23 (25, 29) sts. Beg with a WS row, knit 6 rows (3 ridges of garter st), inc 6 (4, 6) sts evenly across last row. (29, 29, 35 sts)

Purl 1 row, knit 1 row.

Beg pat (WS): P1, k3, *p3, k3; rep from * to last st, end p1.

Row 2: K1, p1, k1B, p1, *k3, p1, k1B, p1; rep from * to last st, end k1.

Work in established pat, *at the same time*, beg on Row 4, inc 1 st at each edge [every 8th row] 2 (3, 3) times. (33, 35, 41 sts)

Work even until sleeve measures 6 (7, 8) inches or desired length to underarm. Mark each end of last row, then work even for approx ¾ inch more, ending with Row 4 or 8. Bind off knitwise on WS.

Assembly

Bind off front and back shoulders tog, using 3-Needle Bind-Off, page 26.

Front band

Note: A circular needle is recommended to accommodate the sts more easily; do not join, work back and forth in rows.

With RS facing, beg at lower right front corner, pick up and knit 3 sts across end of lower border, 2 sts for every 3 rows along front edge to neck, place marker, M1, k3 (6, 10) sts from holder, place marker, pick up and knit 7 (7, 8) sts along neck edge, k17 (17, 19) back neck sts from holder, pick up and knit 7 (7, 8) sts along left neck edge, place marker, k3 (6, 10) sts from holder, M1, place marker, pick up and knit sts along left front edge to match right edge, end with 3 sts across lower border.

Row 1 (WS): Sl 1, knit across.

Row 2: Sl 1, knit to first marker, yo (buttonhole), sl marker, k1, M1, knit to 1 st before next marker, knit next 2 sts tog, replacing marker after resulting st, knit to 1 st before next marker, *at the same time*, dec 2 sts across back neck, knit next 2 sts tog, replacing marker before resulting st, knit to 1 st before last marker, M1, k1, M1, knit to end.

Row 3: Rep Row 1.

Row 4: Sl 1, knit to first marker, M1, sl marker, k1, M1, knit to 1 st before next marker, knit next 2 sts tog, replacing marker after resulting st, knit to 1 st before next marker, knit next 2 sts tog, replacing marker before resulting st, knit to 1 st before last marker, M1, k1, M1, knit to end.

Row 5: Rep Row 1.

Bind off all sts purlwise on RS.

Sew sleeve tops into armholes; match markers to sides of body and sew sleeve edges to bound-off sts of body. Sew sleeve and body seams.

Sew button on left front band to match buttonhole.

Block lightly.

Cube

Finished Measurement
Approx 5 inches square

Materials
Worsted weight acrylic yarn (241 yds/100g per ball): 1 ball each aqua, light yellow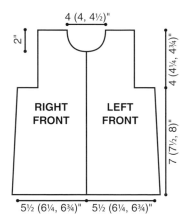
Worsted weight acrylic yarn (170 yds/85g per ball): 1 ball baby variegated
Size 6 (4mm) needles or size needed to obtain gauge
Polyester fibrefill

Gauge
17 sts and 24 rows = 4 inches/10cm in pat
To save time, take time to check gauge.

Cube Panel
Make 1 of each colour

Cast on 22 sts and work in garter st for 21 ridges, ending with a WS row. Purl 1 row, marking each end for corner with a scrap of contrasting yarn. Knit 1 row, inc 1 st. (23 sts)

Beg with a knit row, work 3 rows in St st.

Beg pat (WS): P1, k3, *p3, k3; rep from * to last st, end p1.

Row 2: K1, p1, k1B, p1, *k3, p1, k1B, p1; rep from * to last st, end k1.

Continue to work in established pat, working [Rows 1–8] 3 times.

Knit 1 row (WS), dec 1 st, then bind off purlwise on RS.

Assembly
Sew panels into a cube, matching markers to corners, and leaving approx 3 inches of last edge open. Stuff to desired firmness, complete seam and fasten off securely. ■

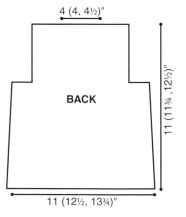

STRIPED HENLEY ROMPER SET

Bright colours in a bold, striped design create the colourful appeal in this captivating set.

Designs | Kennita Tully

Skill Level

Romper: ⬛⬛⬜⬜
EASY

Hat: ⬛⬛⬛⬜
INTERMEDIATE

Sizes

Infant 6 (12, 18, 24) months. Instructions are given for smallest size, with larger sizes in parentheses. When only 1 number is given, it applies to all sizes.

Finished Measurements

Cuff to cuff measurement: 18¾ (20½, 22, 23¼) inches
Length: 21 (22½, 24, 25½) inches
Hat circumference: 15 (16½, 18½) inches

Materials

DK weight mercerized cotton/acrylic blend yarn (136 yds/50g per ball): 3 (3, 4, 4) balls bright blue (A), 2 (3, 3, 3) balls canary yellow (B)
Size 4 (3.5mm) straight and 16-inch circular needles
Size 5 (3.75 mm) double-pointed, 16- and 24-inch circular needles or size needed to obtain gauge
Stitch holders
Tapestry needle
½ (½, ⅔, ⅔) yd snap tape
Sewing machine or hand-sewing needle and matching thread

Gauge

22 sts and 32 rows = 4 inches/10cm in St st with larger needles
To save time, take time to check gauge.

Stripe Sequence

Work in St st stripes of 8 rows A, then 8 rows B.

Romper

Back

Beg at left leg with smaller needles and B, cast on 22 (22, 24, 28) sts.

Work in Stripe pat, inc 1 st each end of 7th (5th, 5th, 5th) row.

[Inc 1 st every 8th (6th, 6th, 6th) row] 4 (7, 8, 8) times at inside of leg and *at the same time,* [inc 1 st every 8th (6th, 6th, 6th) row] 4 (6, 3, 3) times at outside seam.

Continue to [inc 1 st at outside seam only every 0 (0, 8, 8) rows] 0 (0, 4, 4) times. (32, 37, 41, 45 sts)

Work even until leg measures 6 (6½, 7, 7½) inches, ending with a WS row.

Cut yarn, place sts on holder.

Right Leg

Work as for left leg, reversing shaping. Do not cut yarn.

Join for body

Next row: Keeping to colour sequence, knit sts of right leg, sl sts of left leg from holder to LH needle, knit to end of row. (64, 74, 82, 90 sts)

Body

[Inc 1 st each end every 6th row] twice. (68, 78, 86, 94 sts)

Work even until body measures 9 (9½, 10, 10½) inches above crotch, ending with a WS row.

Shape sleeves

Cast on 3 sts at end of next 8 rows. (92, 102, 110, 118 sts)

Work even for 2½ (3, 3½, 4) inches, ending with a WS row.

Shoulder shaping

Bind off 6 (7, 7, 8) sts at beg of next 10 (4, 10, 4) rows, then 5 (6, 6, 7) sts at beg of following 2 (8, 2, 8) rows.

Bind off remaining 22 (26, 28, 30) sts for back neck.

Front

Work as for back, to beg of sleeve shaping.

Divide for placket

Next row (RS): Work across 31 (36, 40, 44) sts, join 2nd ball of yarn and bind off next 6 sts, work to end of row.

Working on both sides simultaneously with separate balls of yarn, cast on 3 sts at end of next 8 rows for sleeve shaping, *at the same time,* work even at placket edge until placket measures 3½ inches.

Shape neck

Bind off at each neck edge 3 sts 1 (1, 1, 2) times, then 2 sts 1 (2, 3, 2) times. [Dec 1 st every other row] 3 (3, 2, 2) times.

At the same time, when sleeve measures same as for back, shape shoulders as for back.

Front Placket

With smaller needles and A, pick up and knit 22 sts along one edge of front opening.

Work even in St st for 20 rows.

Fold placket in half and sew to inside.

Rep for 2nd side.

Sew shoulder seams.

Neck Band

With smaller needles and A, pick up and knit 17 (17, 19, 19) sts along right side of neck, 22 (26, 28, 30) sts along back neck and 17 (17, 19, 19) sts along left side of neck. (56, 60, 66, 68 sts)

Work even in St st for 12 rows.

Bind off loosely.

Fold neck band to inside and sew in place.

Sleeve Cuff

With smaller needles and A, pick up and knit 3 sts for every 4 rows along sleeve edge.

Work even in St st for 18 rows.

Striped Henley Romper Set
Sample projects were knit with
Wildflower DK (51 per cent
mercerized cotton/49 per cent
acrylic) from Plymouth Yarn Co.

Bind off.

Fold cuff in half to inside and sew in place.

Sew sleeve and side seam.

Leg Placket

With smaller needles and A, pick up and knit 3 sts for every 4 rows along front of right leg and same amount along left leg.

Work even in St st for 20 rows.

Bind off.

Fold placket in half to inside and sew in place.

Rep for back leg placket.

Cuff
Left Leg

With smaller needles and A, pick up and knit 7 sts along front placket, 1 st in each cast-on st of leg. Do not pick up sts in back placket.

Work even in St st for 28 rows.

Bind off.

Rep for right leg, picking up sts along leg first, then along placket.

Finishing

Sew snap tape to leg plackets, beg and ending above cuff. Do not sew tape to cuffs.

Sew leg cuff seam.

Fold cuff in half to inside and sew in place.

Sew lower end of back leg placket to top of cuff.

Sew snap tape to neck placket.

Overlap lower edges of placket and sew to romper body, joining both plackets.

Hat

Body

With smaller circular needle and A, cast on 84 (90, 102) sts.

Join without twisting, pm between first and last st.

Work in St st for 1½ inches.

Change to larger needles and B, beg stripe sequence.

Work even in Stripe Pat until 5 rnds of 2nd yellow stripe have been completed.

Beg shaping

Dec Rnd: *K12 (13, 15), k2tog; rep from * around.

Work even for 7 rnds.

Dec Rnd 2: *K11 (12, 14), k2tog; rep from * around.

Work even for 7 rnds.

Dec every 8th rnd as before, having 1 less st between each dec until 24 sts remain. Change to dpn when necessary.

Next row: K2tog across row. (12 sts)

Cut yarn, leaving an 8-inch end.

Draw end through all sts twice and fasten off on inside. ■

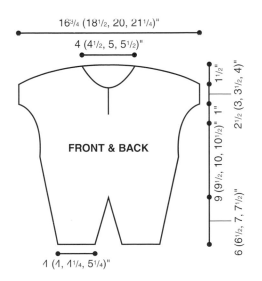

16¾ (18½, 20, 21¼)"

4 (4½, 5, 5½)"

1½"

1"

2½ (3, 3½, 4)"

FRONT & BACK

9 (9½, 10, 10½)"

6 (6½, 7, 7½)"

4 (4, 4¼, 5¼)"

LITTLE BUTTERCUP BABY CAP

This honey of a checked pattern is fun to knit and keeps Baby warm when the weather is cold.

Design | Joyce Messenger

Skill Level
BEGINNER

Finished Measurement
Circumference: Approx 17½ inches

Materials
Worsted weight acrylic yarn (315 yds/6 oz per ball): 1 ball soft yellow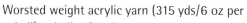
Size 5 (3.75mm) needles or size needed to obtain gauge

Gauge
18 sts = 4 inches/10cm in pat
To save time, take time to check gauge.

Cap

Cast on 78 sts.

Ribbing
Row 1: K2, *p2, k2; rep from * across.

Row 2: P2, *k2, p2; rep from * across.

Rep Rows 1 and 2 until ribbing measures 2 inches.

Body
Rows 1–4: *K3, p3; rep from * across.

Rows 5–8: *P3, k3; rep from * across.

Work Rows 1–8 until piece measures 7 inches.

Next row: *K1, p1; rep from * across.

[Rep last row] 3 times.

Shape top
Row 1: *K2tog, p2tog; rep from * across. (39 sts)

Row 2: *K2tog, p2tog; rep from * to last 3 sts, k2tog, p1. (20 sts)

Row 3: *K1, p1; rep from * across.

Rows 4–6: Rep Row 3.

Row 7: *K2tog, p2tog; rep from * across. (10 sts)

Fasten off, leaving a 24-inch tail. Weave end through sts. Pull to secure.

Sew side seam, reversing seam for cuff.

Make 3-inch pompom following instructions on page 82. Sew to top of hat. ■

Little Buttercup Baby Cap
Sample project was knit with
Simply Soft (100 per cent acrylic)
from Caron International.

BIRD'S-EYE STRIPES

An easy texture pattern and a touch of colour combine for a pullover to keep your little one cozy.

Design | E. J. Slayton

Skill Level
EASY

Sizes

Child 12 months (18 months, 2T, 4T). Instructions are given for smallest size, with larger sizes in parentheses. When only 1 number is given, it applies to all sizes.

Finished Measurements

Chest: 21 (22, 24, 26) inches
Length: 11 (12, 13½, 14½) inches

Materials

DK weight cotton yarn (249 yds/125g per ball):
  2 (2, 2, 3) balls azure (MC), 1 ball cream (CC)
Size 4 (3.5mm) needles or size needed to obtain gauge
Stitch holders & stitch markers
2 buttons

3 LIGHT

Gauge

22 sts = 4 inches/10cm in St st
19 sts = 4 inches/10cm in pat
To save time, take time to check gauge.

Special Abbreviation

K1B (knit 1 in row below):
  K1 in st 1 row below next st on LH needle, sl both sts off needle. (Fig. 1)

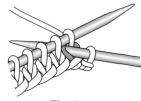

Fig. 1

Pattern Stitch

Bird's-Eye (odd number of sts)

Row 1 (WS): P1, knit to last st, end p1.

Row 2: K1, *k1B, k1; rep from * across.

Row 3: Rep Row 1.

Row 4: K2, *k1B, k1; rep from * to last 3 sts, end k1B, k2.

Rep Rows 1–4 for pat.

Stripe Sequence

6 rows MC
*2 rows CC
4 rows MC
2 rows CC
8 rows MC
2 rows CC
8 rows MC
Rep from * throughout.

Pattern Notes

Keep 1 selvage stitch at each edge in Stockinette stitch; selvage stitch is the easiest place to count rows.

When working sleeve increases, work increase 1 stitch in from edge. Increase on Wrong Side by knitting 1 in top of stitch in the row below the stitch on the needle.

Bird's-Eye Stripes
Sample project was knit with
Super 10 DK (100 per cent
cotton) from S.R. Kertzer.

Back

With MC, cast on 49 (53, 57, 61) sts.

Row 1 (WS): P1, *k1, p1; rep from * across.

Row 2: K1, *p1, k1; rep from * across.

Rep Rows 1 and 2 until ribbing measures approx 1½ (1½, 1½, 2) inches, ending with a RS row.

Beg with Row 1, work in pat and stripe sequence until back measures 7 (7½, 8½, 9) inches from beg, ending with a WS row.

Shape underarms

Maintaining established Bird's-Eye pat and Stripe Sequence, bind off 7 sts at beg of next 2 rows. (35, 39, 43, 47 sts)

Work even until armhole measures 4 (4½, 5, 5½) inches, ending with a WS row. Mark centre 17 (17, 19, 19) sts for back neck, place neck and right shoulder sts on holders.

Left shoulder tab

Mark each end of row. With MC, work in k1, p1 rib on 9 (11, 12, 14) shoulder sts until tab measures 1 inch from marked row.

Bind off in pat.

Front

Work as for back including underarm shaping, until armhole measures 1½ (2, 2½, 3) inches, ending with a WS row.

Shape neck

Maintaining established Bird's-Eye pat and Stripe Sequence, work across first 12 (14, 16, 18) sts; place next

11 sts on holder for front neck; attach 2nd ball of yarn, work across rem 12 (14, 16 18) sts.

Working both sides at once with separate balls of yarn, dec 1 st at each neck edge [every RS row] 3 (3, 4, 4) times by working in pat to last 3 sts, k2tog, k1; k1, ssk, complete row in pat.

When decs are completed, work even on rem 9 (11, 12, 14) sts until front measures same as back at shoulder, ending with a WS row.

Bind off right front and back shoulder sts tog using 3-Needle Bind-Off, page 26.

Left shoulder tab

Mark each end of row.

Row 1 (RS): With MC, k1, [p1, k1] 1 (2, 2, 3) times, yo, k2tog, [p1, k1] twice, k0 (0, 1, 1).

Row 2: P1 (1, 2, 2), *k1, p1; rep from * across.

Row 3: *K1, p1; rep from *, end k1 (1, 2, 2).

Rows 4 and 5: Rep Rows 2 and 3.

Bind off in pat, leaving last st on needle; do not cut yarn.

Neck band

With RS facing, beg at left shoulder tab and counting st on needle as first st, pick up and knit 5 sts across end of shoulder tab, 11 sts along left neck edge, knit 11 sts from front neck holder, pick up and knit 11 sts along right neck edge, knit 17 (17, 19, 19) sts from back neck holder, pick up and knit 4 sts across edge of back shoulder tab. (59, 59, 61, 61 sts)

Row 1 (WS): P2, *k1, p1; rep from * to last st, end p1.

Row 2: K2, p2tog, yo, *p1, k1; rep from * to last st, end k1.

Row 3: Rep Row 1.

Row 4: K2, *p1, k1; rep from * to last st, end k1.

Row 5: Rep Row 1.

Bind off in pat.

Sleeves

With MC, cast on 23 (25, 27, 29) sts and work in rib as for back, ending with a RS row.

Beg Bird's-Eye pat and stripe sequence, *at the same time*, keeping 1 selvage st at each edge in St st throughout, inc 1 st at each edge [every 4th row] 4 (4, 6, 6) times, then [every 6th row] 4 (5, 5, 6) times. (39, 43, 49, 53 sts)

Work even in established Bird's-Eye pat and stripe sequence until sleeve measures 7½ (8, 8½, 9) inches from beg.

Mark each end of row, then work even for an additional 1½ inches, ending with a RS row.

Bind off knitwise on WS.

Assembly

Pin or baste left shoulder tabs in place, matching markers.

Sew top of sleeve to armhole edge. Matching markers to edge of body, sew top of sleeve to bound-off sts at underarm. Sew sleeve and body underarm seams, matching stripes.

Sew buttons opposite buttonholes. Sew armhole edge of back shoulder tab in place. ■

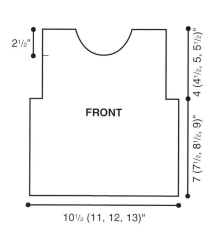

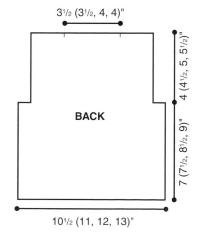

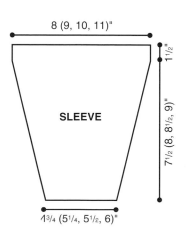

BABY BRIGHT SWEATER

Created by knitting in the round, these bright colours are as happy as a baby!

Design | Carol May

Skill Level ◗■□▭
EASY

Sizes
Infant 3 (6, 12, 24) months. Instructions are given for smallest size, with larger sizes in parentheses. When only 1 number is given, it applies to all sizes.

Finished Measurements
Chest: 20 (21, 22, 23) inches
Length: 10 (10½, 11½, 13) inches

Materials
DK weight acrylic yarn (152 yds/50g per ball):
  2 balls variegated (A), 1 ball each bright lilac (B) and peacock (C)
Size 3 (3.25mm) needles
Size 5 (3.75mm) set of 5 double-pointed and straight needles or size needed to obtain gauge
Stitch markers
Stitch holder
3 (3, 4, 5) small buttons

Gauge
22 sts and 42 rows = 4 inches/10cm in seed st with larger needles
To save time, take time to check gauge.

Pattern Notes
Body of sweater is worked in the round on double-pointed needles to underarm, then divided for front and back yokes.
Colour pattern with variegated yarn varies for each size.

Pattern Stitch
Seed St (in rnds)

Rnd 1: *K1, p1; rep from * around.

Rnd 2: *P1, k1; rep from * around.

Rep Rnds 1 and 2 for pat.

Seed St (for yoke and sleeves)

Row 1: *K1, p1; rep from * across.

Row 2: *P1, k1; rep from * across.

Rep Rows 1 and 2 for pat.

Body
With A and dpn, cast on 110 (116, 122, 126) sts. Divide sts evenly on 4 needles, place marker at beg of rnd.

With 5th needle, work Seed St pat for 1½ inches.

Continue in Seed St pat in following Colour Sequence:

Baby Bright Sweater
Sample project was knit with Look At Me! DK (100 per cent acrylic) from Patons.

*With B, work 2 rows.

With A, work 6 rows.

Rep from * until piece measures 5½ (5½, 6, 7) inches.

Divide for back and front yokes

Change to larger straight needle and B. Bind off first 7 (8, 7, 7) sts for armhole; knit across 48 (50, 54, 56) sts; place rem 55 (58, 61, 63) sts on holder.

Back yoke

With B, work garter st on 48 (50, 54, 56) sts until 3 garter ridges are completed. With C, work 2 rows of seed st. With B, work 2 rows of seed st. Continue to alternate colours until piece measures 10 (10½, 11½, 13) inches from beg.

Bind off all sts.

Front yoke

With B, bind off first 7 (8, 7, 7) sts from holder. Work in garter st on 48 (50, 54, 56) sts for 3 ridges, ending with a RS row.

Right front yoke

Work Seed St and colour sequence as for back yoke across first 22 (22, 24, 26) sts, turn, leaving rem sts for later.

Continue in pat until front measures 2½ (3, 4, 5½) inches from garter ridges.

Shape neck

Bind off 6 sts at neck edge. Continue in pat, dec 1 st at neck edge by k2tog every row until 12 sts rem.

Continue until same length as back.

Bind off all sts.

Left front yoke

Attach yarn at end of right yoke, bind off centre 4 (6, 6, 4) sts. Work left side to match right, binding off 6 sts at neck edge and dec by ssk.

Sew shoulder seams.

Placket

With C and smaller needle, RS facing, pick up and knit 18 (21, 26, 34) sts from right side of placket opening. Work 2 (3, 3, 2) garter ridges, ending with a RS row.

Next row: [K4, k2tog, yo] 3 (3, 4, 5) times, knit rem sts.

Continue in garter st until there are 5 (6, 6, 5) ridges.

Bind off all sts.

Work left placket edge as above, omitting buttonholes.

Neck band

With C and smaller needle, pick up and k 74 (76, 78, 80) sts evenly around neck. Work 3 ridges of garter st.

Bind off all sts.

Sleeves

With smaller needle, and C, cast on 36 sts. Work in garter st for 3 ridges.

Change to larger needles and A, work Seed St pat in colour sequence as for body. *At the same time*, inc 1 st on each side of first row, then every 3rd row until there are 50 (58, 64, 70) sts.

Work even until sleeve measures 5½ (6, 6½, 7½) inches from beg. Change to B and work in garter st for 3 ridges.

Bind off all sts.

Assembly

Sew tops of sleeves to yoke, sew underarm seams.

Lapping right side over left, sew ends of plackets to bound-off sts. Sew buttons in place. ■

ADORABLE BABY HOODIE

For a delightful gift, knit our baby jacket in a simple lace pattern and set it off with beautiful small buttons.

Design | Nazanin S. Fard

Skill Level

EASY

Size
Newborn to 6 months

Finished Measurements
Chest: 20 inches
Length: 10 inches
Sleeve length: 6 inches

Materials
Worsted weight cotton yarn (120 yds/71g per ball): 4 balls lavender
Size 8 (5mm) 29-inch circular needle or size needed to obtain gauge
Stitch markers
Stitch holders
Size H/8 (5mm) crochet hook
5 (⅝-inch) buttons #32609 from JHB International

Gauge
20 sts and 28 rows = 4 inches/10cm in St st
To save time, take time to check gauge.

Pattern Stitch
Eyelet & Garter Rib (multiple of 6 sts + 3)

Row 1 (RS): P3, *k1, yo, k2tog, p3; rep from * across.

Row 2: K3, *p3, k3; rep from * across.

Row 3: Knit across.

Row 4: Purl across.

Rep Rows 1–4 for pat.

Hoodie
Cast on 95 sts.

Rows 1–4: Knit across.

Row 5: K4, place marker, work Row 1 of pat to last 4 sts, place marker, end k4.

Rows 6–32: Keeping 4 sts at each side in garter st, work in established pat.

Row 33 (buttonhole row): K1, yo, k2tog, complete row as set.

Row 34–41: Work in established pat.

Shape armholes
Maintaining established pat throughout, work first 25 sts (right front), bind off 3 sts for armhole; work next 39 sts (back), bind off 3 sts for armhole; work rem 25 sts (left front). Place back and right front sts on holders.

Left Front

Work in pat to end of Row 55.

Shape neck

Row 56: Bind off 5 sts, work to end of row.

Rows 57 and 59: Work in pat to last 2 sts, end ssk.

Rows 58 and 60: Bind off 3 sts, work in pat across. (12 sts rem at end of Row 60)

Rows 61–67: Work in pat.

Bind off all sts.

Right Front

Sl right front sts back to needle, join yarn and work in pat to end of Row 56.

Shape neck

Row 57: Bind off 5 sts, work to end of row.

Rows 58 and 60: Work in pat to last 2 sts, end k2tog.

Rows 59 and 61: Bind off 3 sts, work in pat across. (12 sts rem at end of Row 60)

Rows 62–68: Work in pat.

Bind off all sts.

Back

Row 43–68: Work even in pat.

Bind off 12 sts for right shoulder, k15 sts, bind off last 12 sts for left shoulder, leaving back neck sts on needle.

Hood

Work in pat across 15 back neck sts for 38 rows.

Using cable cast-on, cast on 24 sts on each side. (63 sts)

Work in pat for 32 rows. Knit 4 rows. Bind off all sts loosely.

Sleeves

Cast on 27 sts. Knit 4 rows.

Beg pat, and *at the same time*, inc 1 st at each edge [every 8th row] 3 times. (33 sts)

Work even in pat to end of Row 44. Bind off all sts.

Assembly

Sew shoulder seams.

Sew side seams of hood. Sew bottom edge of hood along neck edge.

Sew sleeve seams, set sleeves into armholes.

With crochet hook and beg at centre back, work 1 rnd of single crochet around bottom edge, front edges and hood. Fasten off.

Sew buttons on left front to match buttonholes. ■

Adorable Baby Hoodie
Sample project was knit with
Sugar'n Cream (100 per cent
cotton) from Lily.

BUBBLEGUM BABY TRIO

Small Fair Isle motifs are used to create the colourful design in this three-piece set for Baby.

Designs | Sandi Prosser

Skill Level
INTERMEDIATE

Sizes
Infant 6 (12, 18, 24) months. Instructions are given for smallest size, with larger sizes in parentheses. When only 1 number is given, it applies to all sizes.

Finished Measurements
Chest: 20 (22, 24, 26) inches
Length: 9½ (10½, 11½, 13) inches
Pants Inseam: 6 (7½, 8, 9) inches

Materials
DK weight mercerized cotton/acrylic blend yarn (136 yds/50g per ball):
Jacket and Hat:
> 2 (2, 2, 3) balls lilac (MC)
> 2 balls seafoam (A)
> 2 balls aqua (B)
> 1 ball each white (C), bubblegum (D)

Pants:
> 1 (1, 2, 2) balls lilac (MC)
> 1 ball each seafoam (A), aqua (B), white (C), bubblegum (D)

Size 3 (3.25mm) needles
Size 6 (4.25mm) needles or size needed to obtain gauge
Size E/4 crochet hook
1 (⅝-inch) button
1 yd (½-inch) elastic
3-inch piece of cardboard

Gauge
24 sts and 32 rows = 4 inches/10cm in St st with larger needles
To save time, take time to check gauge.

Stripe Pattern
Work in St st in the following colour sequence:
6 rows bubblegum, 4 rows MC, 2 rows white, 6 rows seafoam, 4 rows white, 6 rows aqua, 2 rows MC, 4 rows bubblegum, 2 rows aqua, 4 rows seafoam, 6 rows MC, 4 rows white.

Pattern Note
Carry colour not in use loosely across back of work.

Jacket

Back
With MC and smaller needles, cast on 55 (61, 67, 73) sts.

Beg with a WS row, work in garter st for 5 rows, inc 6 sts evenly on last WS row. (61, 67, 73, 79 sts)

Change to larger needles.

Bubblegum Baby Trio
Sample projects were knit with Wildflower DK (51 per cent mercerized cotton/49 per cent acrylic) from Plymouth Yarn Co

Referring to Chart A, beg and end as indicated for chosen size, work even until back measures 5 (5½, 6¼, 7½) inches, ending with a WS row.

Shape armhole
Bind off 3 sts at beg of next 2 rows.

[Dec 1 st each end every other row] 3 times. (49, 55, 61, 67 sts)

Work even until armhole measures 4½ (5, 5¼, 5½) inches, ending with a WS row.

Shape neck
Next row (RS): Bind off 14 (15, 17, 20) sts, work across next 21 (25, 27, 27) sts and sl to holder, bind off rem 14 (15, 17, 20) sts.

Left Front
With MC and smaller needles, cast on 27 (30, 33, 36) sts.

Work in garter st as for back, inc 3 sts evenly across last WS row. (30, 33, 36, 39 sts)

Change to larger needles.

Referring to Chart A, beg and end as indicated for chosen size, work even until front measures same as for back to underarm, ending with a WS row.

Shape armhole
Bind off 3 sts at beg of next row.

[Dec 1 st at arm edge every other row] 3 times. (24, 27, 30, 33 sts)

Work even until armhole measures 2½ (3, 3¼, 3½) inches, ending with a RS row.

Neck shaping
Next row: Bind off 6 sts, work to end of row.

[Dec 1 st at neck edge every row] 3 (3, 5, 5) times, then [every other row] 1 (3, 2, 2) times. (14, 15, 17, 20 sts)

Work even until armhole measures same as for back armhole.

Bind off.

Right Front

Work as for left front, reversing shaping.

Sleeves

With smaller needles and MC, cast on 35 (35, 37, 39) sts.

Work in garter st as for back, inc 6 sts evenly on last WS row. (41, 41, 43 sts)

Change to larger needles.

Referring to Chart B, beg and end as indicated for chosen size, [inc 1 st each end every 4th row] 11 (13, 14, 15) times, working added sts into pat. (57, 61, 65, 69 sts)

Work even in established pat until sleeve measures 5½ (6½, 7½, 8½) inches, ending with a WS row.

Shape cap

Bind off 3 sts at beg of next 2 rows.

[Dec 1 st at each end every other row] 3 times. (45, 49, 53, 57 sts)

Bind off.

Sew shoulder seams.

Neck Band

With RS facing, using MC and smaller needles, pick up and knit 25 (25, 27, 27) sts along right front edge, k19 (21, 25, 27) sts of back neck, pick up and knit 25 (25, 27, 27) sts along left front edge. (69, 71, 79, 81 sts)

Work 4 rows in garter st.

Bind off knitwise on WS.

Front Edgings

With RS facing, using MC and smaller needles, pick up and knit 52 (54, 58, 64) sts along front edge.

Knit 2 rows.

Bind off knitwise on WS.

Finishing

Attach MC to top of neck, at right edge for girl or left edge for boy.

With crochet hook, ch 10, sk 2 bound-off sts, sl st in next st. Fasten off.

Sew sleeves into armholes.

Sew sleeve and side seams.

Sew on button.

Pants

Legs

With MC and smaller needles, cast on 35 (39, 43, 45) sts.

Work in k1, p1 ribbing for 1½ inches, inc 34 (38, 42, 44) sts evenly on last WS row. (69, 75, 85, 89 sts)

Change to larger needles.

Working in Stripe pat, [inc 1 st each end of needle every 4th row] 7 (8, 7, 7) times. (83, 91, 99, 103 sts)

Work even until leg measures 6 (7½, 9, 10½) inches, ending with a WS row.

COLOUR KEY
- Lilac (MC)
- Seafoam (A)
- Aqua (B)
- White (C)
- Bubblegum (D)

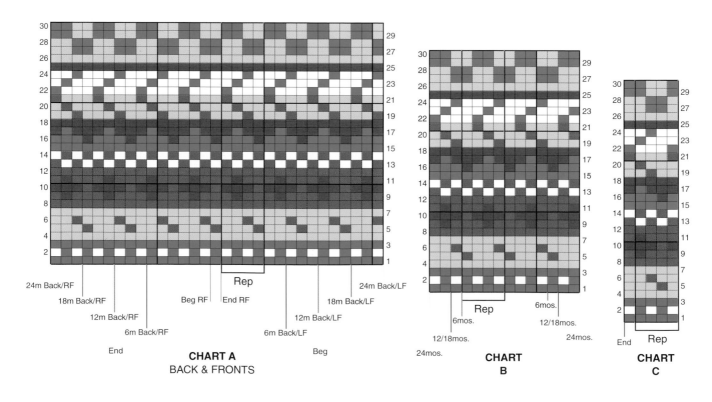

CHART A
BACK & FRONTS

CHART B

CHART C

Shape crotch

Bind off 3 sts at beg of next 2 rows. [Dec 1 st each end every other row] twice.

Cut yarn; sl sts to holder.

Work 2nd leg as for first; do not cut yarn.

Next row: With appropriate colour, k73 (81, 89, 93) sts on needle, sl sts from holder to LH needle and knit them. (146, 162, 178, 186 sts)

Work even in Stripe pat until pants measures 6½ (7, 7½, 8) inches above bound-off crotch sts, ending with a WS row. Change to MC.

Next row: K1 (2, 1, 2), *k2tog, k1, rep from * across, end last rep k1. (98, 108, 118, 124 sts)

Change to smaller needles.

Work even in k1, p1 ribbing for 1½ inches.

Bind off loosely in ribbing.

Finishing

Sew centre front and back seams.

Sew leg seams.

Fold waistband in half to wrong side and sew loosely in position leaving an opening to insert elastic.

Cut elastic to desired waist measurement and insert in casing.

Sew ends of elastic tog securely.

Sew opening of waistband tog.

Hat

With MC and smaller needles, cast on 93 (97, 101, 105) sts.

Beg with a WS row, work in garter st for 7 rows.

Change to larger needles.

Referring to Chart C, work even in pat until hat measures 5½ (6, 6½, 7) inches.

Bind off.

Finishing

Fold hat in half.

Sew top and side seam.

Tassels

Make 2

Wrap MC around cardboard approximately 50 times. Tie one end; cut other end.

Tie another strand tightly around top of tassel, about 1 inch below first tie.

Sew 1 tassel to each corner of hat. ■

MARY JANE SOCKS

Baby girl's footsies will have special-occasion style in these clever socks.

Design | Kathy Wesley

Skill Level

EASY

Finished Measurement

4-inch-long foot

Materials

Worsted weight acrylic yarn (165 yds/3 oz per
    ball): 1 ball each white (A) and black (B)
Size 5 (3.75mm) needles or size needed to obtain gauge
Size H/8 (5mm) crochet hook (for strap)
Stitch holders
2 (¼-inch) pearl buttons
Sewing needle and matching thread

Gauge

20 sts and 32 rows = 4 inches/10cm in St st
To save time, take time to check gauge.

Cuff

With A, cast on 38 sts.

Row 1 (WS): K2, *p2, k2; rep from * across.

Row 2: P2, *k2, p2; rep from * across.

Rep Rows 1 and 2 until ribbing measures 2 inches,
ending with a WS row.

Sock

Row 1 (RS): K2tog, [k4, k2tog] 6 times. (31 sts)

Row 2: Purl across.

Row 3: Knit across.

Row 4: Purl across.

Rows 5 and 6: Rep Rows 3 and 4.

Instep

Row 1 (RS): K21, sl rem 10 sts to a holder.

Row 2: P11, sl rem 10 sts to a holder.

Row 3: K11.

Row 4: P11.

Rep Rows 3 and 4 until instep measures 1½ inches,
ending with a WS row. Cut A.

Foot

Holding with RS facing and instep to left, with B, knit
across 10 sts on first holder, pick up and knit 12 sts along
side edge of instep, knit across 11 instep sts, pick up and
knit 12 sts along other side of instep, knit 10 sts from 2nd
holder. (55 sts)

Mary Jane Socks
Sample projects were knit with Simply Soft (100 per cent acrylic) from Caron International.

Knit 9 rows.

Sole

Row 1 (RS): K4, k2tog, k14, k2tog, k11, k2tog, k14, k2tog, k4. (51 sts)

Rows 2, 4, 6 and 8: Knit.

Row 3: K3, k2tog, k14, k2tog, k9, k2tog, k14, k2tog, k3. (47 sts)

Row 5: K2, k2tog, k14, k2tog, k7, k2tog, k14, k2tog, k2. (43 sts)

Row 7: K1, k2tog, k14, k2tog, k5, k2tog, k14, k2tog, k1. (39 sts)

Row 9: K2tog, k14, k2tog, k3, k2tog, k14, k2tog. (35 sts)

Bind off, leaving a long end for sewing.

Strap

Note: If not familiar with crochet ch (ch) and single crochet (sc), see sidebar at right.

With B and crochet hook, ch 10. Sc in 2nd ch from hook and in each rem ch. Fasten off.

Finishing

With tapestry needle, sew bottom and back seam.

Tack each end of strap to bootie at ankle. Sew button to end of strap through all thicknesses. ■

Crochet Basics

Chain Stitch (ch)

Begin by making a slip knot on the hook. Bring the yarn over the hook from back to front and draw through the loop on the hook.

Chain Stitch

For each additional chain stitch, bring the yarn over the hook from back to front and draw through the loop on the hook.

Single Crochet (sc)

Insert the hook in the second chain through the center of the V. Bring the yarn over the hook from back to front.

Draw the yarn through the chain stitch and onto the hook.

Again bring yarn over the hook from back to front and draw it through both loops on hook.

For additional rows of single crochet, insert the hook under both loops of the previous stitch instead of through the center of the V as when working into the chain stitch.

BABY'S FIRST EASTER

Baby will be the hit of the Easter parade in a matching cardigan and hat.

Designs | Scarlet Taylor

Skill Level
EASY

Sizes

Cardigan: Infant 3 (6, 9–12, 18–24) months
Hat: Infant 0–3 (6–12, 18–24) months
Instructions are given for smallest size, with larger sizes in parentheses. When only 1 number is given, it applies to all sizes.

Finished Measurements

Cardigan Chest: 20 (22, 24, 26) inches
Length: 8½ (9½, 10½, 12) inches
Hat Circumference: 15 (16½, 18) inches
Length: 5½ (5½, 6½) inches

Materials

Super bulky weight yarn (38 yds/50g per ball):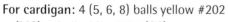
    For cardigan: 4 (5, 6, 8) balls yellow #202 (MC), 1 ball white #201 (CC)
    For hat: 1 ball yellow #202 (MC), few yds white #201 (CC)
Size 13 (9mm) straight and (2) double-pointed needles
Size 15 (10mm) needles or size needed to obtain gauge
1 (1-inch) button, La Mode #4764

Gauge

8 sts and 12 rows = 4 inches/10cm in St st with larger needles
To save time, take time to check gauge.

Special Abbreviation

M1 (Make 1): Insert LH needle under horizontal thread between st just worked and next st, k1-tbl.

Pattern Note

Work buttonhole band on right front for girl's cardigan, and on left front for boy.

Cardigan

Back

With smaller needles and MC, cast on 20 (22, 24, 26) sts.

Work even in garter st until back measures 1 inch from beg, ending with a WS row.

Change to larger needles and St st.

Work even until back measures 7 (8, 9, 10½) inches from beg, ending with a WS row.

Shape shoulders

Bind off 3 (3, 4, 4) sts at beg of next 2 rows, then 2 (3, 3, 4) sts at beg of following 2 rows.

Bind off rem 10 sts for back neck.

Left Front

With smaller needles and MC, cast on 10 (11, 12, 13) sts.

Work even in garter st until front measures 1 inch from beg, ending with a WS row.

Change to larger needles and St st.

Work even until back measures 7 (8, 8½, 9½) inches from beg, ending with a RS row.

Shape neck

Bind off at neck edge [3 sts] once, then [2 sts] once.

Work even until front measures same as for back to shoulder.

Bind off 3 (3, 4, 4) sts at arm edge, work 1 row even, then bind off rem 2 (3, 3, 4) sts.

Right Front

With smaller needles and MC, cast on 10 (11, 12, 13) sts.

Work even in garter st until front measures 1 inch from beg, ending with a WS row.

Change to larger needles and St st.

Work even until back measures 7 (8, 8½, 9½) inches from beg, ending with a WS row.

Shape neck

Bind off at neck edge [3 sts] once, then [2 sts] once.

Work even until front measures same as for back to shoulder.

Bind off 3 (3, 4, 4) sts at arm edge, work 1 row even, then bind off rem 2 (3, 3, 4) sts.

Sleeves

With smaller needles and MC, cast on 11 (13, 14, 16) sts.

Work even in garter st until sleeve measures 1 inch from beg, ending with a WS row.

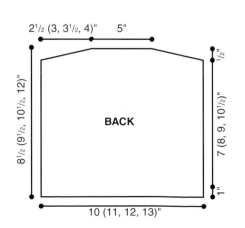

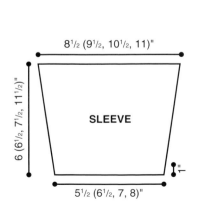

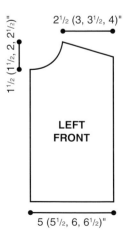

Baby's First Easter

Sample projects were knit with Baby Rimini (85 per cent acrylic/15 per cent wool) from Plymouth Yarn Co.

Change to larger needles and St st.

Inc 1 st by M1 each end of next row, then [every 4th row] 2 (2, 0, 0) times, [every 6th row] 0 (0, 2, 1) times and [every 8th row] 0 (0, 0, 1) times. (17, 19, 20, 22 sts)

Work even until sleeve measures approx 6 (6½, 7½, 11½) inches from beg.

Bind off.

Button Band
With RS facing, using smaller needles and MC, pick up and knit 17 (19, 21, 24) sts evenly along front edge.

Knit 4 rows.

Bind off loosely.

Buttonhole Band
With RS facing, using smaller needles and MC, pick up and knit 17 (19, 21, 24) sts evenly along front edge.

Mark front edge for buttonhole 1 inch below neck.

Knit 1 row.

Buttonhole row (RS): Knit to marker, k2tog, yo, knit to end of row.

Knit 2 rows, working into back of yo on first row.

Bind off loosely.

Collar
Sew shoulder seams.

With smaller needles and CC, beg and ending in picked-up rows of front bands, pick up and knit 29 sts evenly around neck.

Knit 1 row.

Row 2: K1, inc 1 by knitting into front and back of next st, k2, M1, k5, M1, k6, [M1, k5] twice, M1, k2, inc 1 by knitting into front and back of next st, k1. (36 sts)

Row 3: K1, inc 1, k4, [M1, k6] 3 times, M1, k7, M1, k3, inc 1, k1. (43 sts)

Rows 4 and 5: Bind off 1 st, work to end of row. (41 sts)

Row 6: Bind off 2 sts, k14, [M1, k3] 3 times, M1, knit to end of row. (43 sts).

Row 7: Bind off 2 sts, knit to end of row.

Bind off loosely.

Assembly
Measure down from shoulder seam 4½ (4¾, 5, 5½) inches on each side and mark.

Sew sleeves to body between markers.

Sew sleeve and side seams.

Sew on button.

Hat

Border

With smaller needles and MC, cast on 30 (33, 36) sts, leaving a long tail for sewing seam.

Work even in garter st for 1 inch.

Body

Change to larger needles and St st.

Work even until hat measures 4 (4, 5) inches, ending with a WS row.

Shape crown

Row 1 (RS): K2, k2tog, [k1, k2tog] 8 (9, 10) times, k2. (21, 23, 25 sts)

Row 2 and all WS rows: Purl.

Row 3 (RS): K2, [k2tog] 9 (10, 11) times, k1. (12, 13, 14 sts)

Row 5 (RS): [K2tog] 6 (6, 7) times, k0 (1, 0). (6, 7, 7 sts)

Row 7 (Size 0-3 months only): K2tog across. (3 sts)

Row 7 (Size 6-12 and 18-24 months only): K2tog, k3tog, k2tog. (3 sts)

Beg I-Cord knot

Change to CC, slip rem 3 sts onto dpn.

*K3, replace sts to LH needle; rep from * until cord measures 3 inches.

K3tog and fasten off last st.

Assembly

Tie cord into knot.

Sew back seam. ■

INDEX

INDEX

The Best-Dressed Baby

Metric Conversion Charts

METRIC CONVERSIONS

yards	x	.9144	=	metres (m)
yards	x	91.44	=	centimetres (cm)
inches	x	2.54	=	centimetres (cm)
inches	x	25.40	=	millimetres (mm)
inches	x	.0254	=	metres (m)

centimetres	x	.3937	=	inches
metres	x	1.0936	=	yards

INCHES INTO MILLIMETRES & CENTIMETRES (Rounded off slightly)

inches	mm	cm	inches	cm	inches	cm	inches	cm
1/8	3	0.3	5	12.5	21	53.5	38	96.5
1/4	6	0.6	5 1/2	14	22	56	39	99
3/8	10	1	6	15	23	58.5	40	101.5
1/2	13	1.3	7	18	24	61	41	104
5/8	15	1.5	8	20.5	25	63.5	42	106.5
3/4	20	2	9	23	26	66	43	109
7/8	22	2.2	10	25.5	27	68.5	44	112
1	25	2.5	11	28	28	71	45	114.5
1 1/4	32	3.2	12	30.5	29	73.5	46	117
1 1/2	38	3.8	13	33	30	76	47	119.5
1 3/4	45	4.5	14	35.5	31	79	48	122
2	50	5	15	38	32	81.5	49	124.5
2 1/2	65	6.5	16	40.5	33	84	50	127
3	75	7.5	17	43	34	86.5		
3 1/2	90	9	18	46	35	89		
4	100	10	19	48.5	36	91.5		
4 1/2	115	11.5	20	51	37	94		

KNITTING NEEDLES CONVERSION CHART

Canada/U.S.	0	1	2	3	4	5	6	7	8	9	10	10½	11	13	15
Metric (mm)	2	2¼	2¾	3¼	3½	3¾	4	4½	5	5½	6	6½	8	9	10

CROCHET HOOKS CONVERSION CHART

Canada/U.S.	1/B	2/C	3/D	4/E	5/F	6/G	8/H	9/I	10/J	10½/K	N
Metric (mm)	2.25	2.75	3.25	3.5	3.75	4.25	5	5.5	6	6.5	9.0

Skill Levels

BEGINNER

Projects for first-time knitters using basic knit and purl stitches. Minimal shaping.

EASY

Projects using basic stitches, repetitive stitch patterns, simple colour changes and simple shaping and finishing.

INTERMEDIATE

Projects with a variety of stitches, such as basic cables and lace, simple intarsia, double-pointed needles and knitting in the round needle techniques, mid-level shaping and finishing.

EXPERIENCED

Projects using advanced techniques and stitches, such as short rows, Fair Isle, more intricate intarsia, cables, lace patterns and numerous colour changes.

We have a sweet lineup of
cookbooks with plenty more in the oven

www.companyscoming.com

Our website is filled with
all kinds of great information

www.companyscoming.com